Health Translation and Media Communication

Cross-sectoral interaction and cooperation in the communication of nutritional health risks represents a strategic research area among national governments and international health authorities. The key research question this book addresses is whether and how different industrial sectors interact with one another in the communication and industrial utilisation of health research findings. Through the introduction and exploration of large-scale industry news and digital media resources, this book systematically analyses a range of digital news genres and identifies new and growing trends of inter-sectoral interaction around the communication of nutritional health in the Chinese language at both international and national levels. This book argues that cross-sectoral interaction can be explored to identify areas that require policy intervention to increase the efficiency and effectiveness of current health communication and promotion. Inter-sectoral interaction can also provide incentives to develop new social programmes and business models to innovate and transform traditional industrial sectors.

Meng Ji is Associate Professor at the School of Languages and Cultures at The University of Sydney, Australia.

Routledge Studies in Empirical Translation
Series Editor: Meng Ji
The University of Sydney, Australia

Empirical Translation Studies (ETS) represents a rapidly growing field of research which came to the fore in the 1990s. From the early, tentative use of computerised translation to the systematic investigation of large-scale translation corpora by using quantitative/statistical methods, ETS has made substantial progress in the development of solid empirical research methodologies which lie at the heart of the further development of the field. There is a growing volume of research pursued in ETS as corpus translation studies has become a core component of translation studies at the postgraduate and research levels. To offer an appropriate and much-needed outlet for high-quality research in ETS, this proposed book series intends to select and publish the latest translation research around the world, in which the innovative use of corpus materials and related methodologies is essential. An important shared feature of the manuscripts accepted is their original contributions to the advancement of empirical methodologies in translation studies, which includes but is not limited to the quantitative/statistical processing, modelling and interpretation of translation corpora.

For a full list of titles in this series, visit https://www.routledge.com/Routledge-Studies-in-Empirical-Translation/book-series/RSET

Health Translation and Media Communication

A Corpus Study of the Media Communication of Translated Health Knowledge

Meng Ji

Routledge
Taylor & Francis Group

LONDON AND NEW YORK

First published 2018 by Routledge

2 Park Square, Milton Park, Abingdon, Oxfordshire OX14 4RN
52 Vanderbilt Avenue, New York, NY 10017

Routledge is an imprint of the Taylor & Francis Group, an informa business

First issued in paperback 2019

British Library Cataloguing-in-Publication Data
A catalogue record for this book is available from the British Library

Library of Congress Cataloging-in-Publication Data
A catalog record for this book has been requested

ISBN: 978-0-415-79062-8 (hbk)
ISBN: 978-0-367-88701-8 (pbk)

Typeset in Times New Roman
by Apex CoVantage, LLC

Contents

Figures

Tables

1 Study of inter-sectoral interaction using digital language corpora

1.1 Inter-sectoral interaction as an intervention tool

The World Health Organization's policy document on Non-Communicable Diseases Global Monitoring Framework and Targets (2011) highlighted the importance of identifying and focusing on agreed priorities to foster and develop multi-sectoral partnership to ensure that valuable resources are allocated to the highest-need areas of public health. This document points to a critical and urgent gap in the multi-sectoral and international understanding of public health risks which has prevented targeted effort on specific health concerns. Combatting non-communicable diseases provides a focus for collaboration nationally and internationally to develop strategic partnership for greater mutual economic and social benefits. The cross-sectoral nature of the impact of health risks related to non-communicable diseases requires the development of multi-sectoral interaction for effective policy making. The current intra-sectoral nature of health risks communication has been a major limiting factor in the much-needed inter-sectoral collaboration. In this study, the extent that sectors align with or diverge from each other on health risks communication is analysed within the framework of *multi-sectoral interaction*. This is to provide empirical research evidence for enhanced joint action across industrial sectors to tackle the growing epidemic of lifestyle-related health risks and diseases such as diabetes and cardiovascular diseases both domestically and internationally.

Non-communicable diseases and related health risks are strongly correlated with social and economic development. Transition models provide useful analytical tools to explain changes in non-communicable diseases that occur during development from poor to middle-income and rich countries. However, many current transition models have focussed mainly or exclusively on the demographic and economic influences on non-communicable diseases and health risks. This overlooked the mechanism of multi-sectoral interaction, a growing social phenomenon underscored by rapid technological

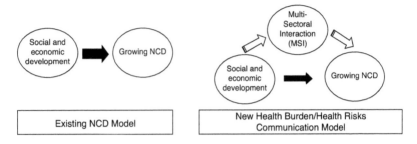

Figure 1.1 Introducing multi-sectoral interaction (MSI) to advance NCD risk management

advances in health information sharing and health knowledge construction, especially digital media, which is instrumental in the framing and communication of non-communicable health risks to different stakeholders and the general public. Figure 1.1 illustrates multi-sectoral interaction as an important tool in the communication about non-communicable diseases. This is particularly relevant for the many developing countries undergoing non-communicable disease transition.

The effective management of non-communicable health risks (nutrition, dietary patterns and sedentary lifestyles, etc.) requires more proactive approaches to reduce exposures to non-communicable health risks and to develop health-promoting cultures that facilitate behaviour modification: purposeful manipulation of lifestyles and consumption habits through social campaigns and movements. This study offers a corpus analysis of the communication, utilisation and framing of health research of non-communicable diseases. Specifically, it analyses the distribution of health terms related to nutritional deficiencies risks in a large global Chinese digital media database during the period 1998–2017. It offers a large-scale empirical analysis of distinct perceptions and sectorally motivated framing of non-communicable health risks in digital discourses and materials produced by different industries.

The quantitative exploration of large amounts of corpus data leads to the construction of multi-sectoral interaction as an analytical instrument. The study aims to demonstrate how multi-sectoral interaction can be a potentially powerful intervention mechanism for effective policy making in tackling growing health risks which require multiple sectoral collaboration. The digital media analysed are published by different societal sectors, industries and media sources containing specialised health research terms in Chinese. The exploration of Chinese digital resources goes beyond national borders by examining and comparing digital resources collected from different countries in order to capture the general lack of multi-sectoral interaction around the communication of non-communicable health risks among global Chinese-speaking societies.

The purpose of this analysis is to provide a benchmark against which to assess the levels of multi-sectoral interaction at the national level (Chapter 3). The almost twenty years between 1998 and 2017 has seen the rapid growth of non-communicable diseases such as type 2 diabetes and cardiovascular diseases as a major global health burden and a top research priority for national and international health authorities.

The cross-national study of multi-sectoral interaction is increasingly pressing, as joint efforts among stakeholders are urgently needed to manage and prevent non-communicable diseases. An in-depth, comparative study of existing multi-sectoral modes in distinct societal systems holds the key to the development of collaboration between governments, academia and industrial partners within and beyond national borders. The urgency of the issue justifies this book's focus as an in-depth and rigorous empirical study supported by large amounts of original Chinese language data to reveal national and sectoral variation and limitation in the development of multi-sectoral interaction.

Multi-sectoral interaction around non-communicable health risks communication in Chinese is a research area that remains largely unexplored, despite its important policy implications. This book expands the knowledge base of this under-explored research field through methodological innovation in the collection and statistical analysis of large amounts of original Chinese data; the construction of multi-sectoral interaction models from textual patterns emerged in multi-sectoral digital materials; the empirical efficiency assessment of multi-sectoral interaction models; and, lastly, recommendations for the translation and communication of health research. The empirical findings presented advance understanding of the mechanism of multi-sectoral interaction as an intervention tool to leverage valuable sectoral resources to deliver targeted and optimised regulatory outcomes.

This study aims to close gaps in the inter-and intra-sectoral communication of non-communicable diseases to build much-needed multi-sectoral cooperation. The exploration of social interaction at intra-and cross-sectoral levels is based on the statistical analysis of the variation and similarity in the distribution of translated health terms and textual segments units extracted from a large Chinese digital database. Two hypotheses are formulated to distinguish between an active or inactive multi-sectoral interaction:

1   Hypothesis 1: When relatively high-level similarities are identified among sectoral materials, an active multi-sectoral interaction model is said to be found among sectors around the communication and utilisation of WHO health research findings regarding the prevention and management of non-communicable health risks.

2   Hypothesis 2: When relatively low-level similarities are identified among sectoral materials, a lack of active multi-sectoral interaction is said to be found among sectors in the communication and utilisation of WHO health research findings regarding the prevention and management of non-communicable health risks.

In order to assess the similarities or differences among the datasets containing industrial information and digital news resources, a systematic corpus analysis of the distribution of translated Chinese health terms across global Chinese-speaking communities and societies is first conducted (Chapter 2). The statistics thus obtained provide the benchmark for the assessment and evaluation of the multi-sectoral interaction extracted from national databases, in this case that of the People's Republic of China.

1.2   Construction of Chinese digital corpora of industry news

In the large-scale digital media analysis of the global Chinese and mainland Chinese digital news, two important types of language corpora were used. One is known as *monolingual comparable corpora,* and the other is *bilingual parallel corpora.* Comparable corpora refer to language databases which share similar structures in terms of the distribution of textual genres included in the databases (Prasad, Webber and Joshi, 2014). The compilation of comparable corpora largely depends on the specific research question. In the current study, a key research question to be addressed is the differences and similarities between global Chinese digital media and Chinese digital media in the communication of nutritional health and the prevention of nutritional health risks highlighted in global health research. For this purpose, the design of the comparable corpora is underlined by the purposeful selection of a range of large industrial sectors that may help identify useful contrastive patterns between the two digital datasets, i.e. the global Chinese digital resources database and the Chinese digital resources database published in the past twenty years.

Specifically, the industrial sectors included in the two comparable Chinese corpora were chosen from the Factiva database, which has a large collection of local and global newspapers, newswires, trade journals, newsletters, magazines and transcripts. A distinctive feature of the Factiva database is that it encompasses global and local news not only in English but also in original national languages such as traditional and simplified Chinese. This has greatly facilitated the compilation of the comparable corpora in Chinese, as the researcher needed only to set up the parameters of the comparable corpora and then let the Factiva database automatically retrieve large amounts of digital resources produced by industrial sectors within a specific timespan in particular Chinese-speaking countries and regions. In the current study, the global Chinese database was set to include all Chinese media publications and licensed digital resources without specification of national origins. This resulted in a very large Chinese digital database with digital materials from global Chinese-speaking societies, countries and communities. By contrast, the Chinese digital database was limited to digital resources published in the People's Republic of China. Both traditional and simplified forms of Chinese writing were included in both databases to reflect the fact that large and influential Chinese and international news agencies and media companies tend to publish in both Chinese writing varieties.

The other language corpora used in this study is known as bilingual parallel corpora. This was created by using the original English resources developed by the World Health Organization on combatting and preventing global nutritional deficiencies, and their official translations to Mandarin Chinese by Chinese translation institutions. The original English database contains WHO nutritional guidelines published between 1990 and 2015, including

1   Diet, Nutrition, and the Prevention of Chronic Diseases: Report of a WHO Study Group (1990) and its translation to Chinese titled 膳食, 营养与慢性病预防 (shàn shí, yíng yǎng yǔ màn xìng bìng yù fáng) by People's Health Press (1992)
2   Complementary Feeding of Young Children in Developing Countries: A Review of Current Scientific Knowledge (1998) and its translation to Chinese titled 发展中国家的幼儿辅食添加: 当代科学知识的综述 (fā zhǎn zhōng guó jiā de yòu ér fǔ shí tiān jiā: dāng dài kē xué zhī shì de zōng shù) led by Dr Shi'an Yin from the Chinese Centre for Disease Control and Prevention, National Institute for Nutrition and Health
3   Preparation and Use of Food-Based Dietary Guidelines: Report of a Joint FAO/WHO Consultation (1998) and its translation to Chinese titled 膳食的合理制备 (shàn shí de hé lǐ zhì bèi) by People's Health Press in Beijing (2000) commissioned by the Chinese Ministry of Health
4   The World Health Report 2002 – Reducing Risks, Promoting Healthy Life (2002) and its Chinese translation titled 2002 年世界卫生报告 '减少风险, 延长健康寿命' (jiǎn shǎo fēng xiǎn, yán cháng jiàn kāng shòu mìng)

5   Diet, Nutrition, and the Prevention of Chronic Diseases: Report of a
    Joint FAO/WHO Consultation (2003) and its translation to Chinese
    titled 膳食, 营养和慢性疾病预防: 世界卫生组织和粮农组织联合专
    家磋商会报告 (shàn shí, yíng yǎng hé màn xìng jí bìng yù fáng: shì jiè
    wèi shēng zǔ zhī hé liáng nóng zǔ zhī lián hé zhuān jiā cuō shāng huì
    bào gào) by China Publishing Group Corporation (CPGC)
6   Global Health Strategy on Diet, Physical Activity and Health (2004)
    and its translation to Chinese titled 饮食、身体活动与健康: 全球
    战略 (yǐn shí, shēn tǐ huó dòng yǔ jiàn kāng: Quán qiú zhàn lüè) by
    CPGC
7   Guidelines on Food Fortification with Micronutrients (2006) by FAO
    and WHO and its Chinese version 微量营养素事物强化指南 trans-
    lated by Department of Food Fortification, Chinese Centre for Disease
    Control and Prevention and published by the Chinese Light Industry
    Press in 2009
8   Global Recommendations on Physical Activity for Health (2010) and
    its translation to Chinese titled 关于身体活动有益健康的全球建议
    by CPGC
9   Guideline: Sugars Intake for Adults and Children (2015) and its Chi-
    nese translation titled 指南: 成人和儿童糖摄入量 (zhǐ nán: chéng rén
    hé ér tóng táng shè rù liàng) by CPGC
10 Information Note about Intake of Sugars Recommended in the WHO
    Guideline for Adults and Children (2015) and its Chinese translation
    titled 关于世卫组织推荐成人和儿童糖摄入量指南的情况说明
    (guan yú shì wèi zǔzhī tuī jiàn chéng rén hé ér tóng táng shè rù liàng
    zhǐnán de qíng kuàng shuō míng) by CPGC.

1.3   Corpus search index of Chinese translations of nutritional health risks

This section introduces the development of a bilingual keyword search
index in English and Chinese. This provides the basis for the following
corpus analysis of the quantitative data extracted from both the global
Chinese language digital database and the mainland Chinese digital database. The bilingual search index facilitates the extraction of news articles
and, more importantly, useful corpus statistics or meta-information indicating the sources and producers of the news content extracted from the
two Chinese-language datasets under comparison. For example, the meta-
information furnished by the Factiva database covers publication dates,
digital media companies and news providers, regions, industries, subjects
and authors' names and affiliations. The range of the meta-information

provided by Factiva enables the exploration of relevant news, its distribution patterns and, more importantly, any potential relationships between different industrial sectors in the communication and foregrounding of specific nutritional health risks over time.

The compilation of the bilingual keyword search index starts with the selection of English keywords. This is guided by the classificatory framework provided by the Global Burden of Disease database, also known as the GBD. The GBD is the most comprehensive worldwide observational epidemiological study to date. It describes mortality and morbidity from major diseases, injuries and risk factors to health at global, national and regional levels. It examines trends from 1990 to the present and makes comparisons across populations which in turn enables understanding of the changing health challenges facing people across the world in the twenty-first century (Murray and Lopez, 1996; Schwartländer, 1997; Ng et al., 2014). The GDB provides a comprehensive classification framework for major global health risks and diseases covering infectious and non-communicable diseases and risk factors; as well as mental and physical diseases and related health risk factors.

This study uses the GBD search tool provided by the Global Health Data Exchange or the GHDx. The GHDx is a data catalogue for demographic, public health and global health data. It was developed by the Institute for Health Metrics and Evaluation (IHME) at the University of Washington and launched to the public in 2011. For the purpose of the current study, which focuses on the communication of nutritional health risks in the digital media, the classification of nutritional deficiencies in the GDB is used as a guideline to the extraction of relevant search keywords. In the GBD, four types of nutritional deficiencies are included: A.6 Nutritional deficiencies; A.6.1 Protein-energy malnutrition; A.6.2 Iodine deficiency; A.6.3 Vitamin (A) deficiency; A.6.4 Iron deficiency or anaemia; and A.6.5 other nutritional deficiencies. For each category of nutrient deficiency, risks and diseases, a number of relevant English expressions and their Chinese translations are provided. The extraction of the English and Chinese terms is based on the bilingual translational database of WHO nutritional guidelines (1990–2015) compiled for the purpose of the present study.

In Table 1.1, careful readers will notice that some original English health terms have been translated into different Chinese terms, for example, 'balanced diet', 'nutrition balance', 'energy balance' and 'bioavailability'. This is related to the study of lexical variation in bilingual health translation. The appendices of this book provide a range of lexical variations in the Chinese official translations of the global nutrition guidelines developed

Table 1.1 Bilingual search index of nutritional deficiency risks

Date	Original english expression	Chinese translation	Pinyin annotation
A.6 Nutritional deficiencies			
1998	balanced diet	平衡 膳食	píng héng shàn shí
2003	balanced diet	均衡 饮食	jūn héng yǐn shí
1990	nutrition balance	营养 均衡	yíng yǎng jūn héng
1998	nutrition balance	营养 平衡	yíng yǎng píng héng
1998	nutrient availability	营养 利用	yíng yǎng lì yòng
1998	nutrient absorption	营养 吸收	yíng yǎng xī shōu
A.6.1 Protein-energy malnutrition			
1998	energy balance	能量 平衡	néng liàng píng héng
1998	energy balance	热量 平衡	rè liàng píng héng
1998	metabolic balance	代谢 平衡	dài xiè píng héng
A.6.2 Iodine deficiency			
1998	iodine deficiency	碘 缺乏	diǎn quē fá
A.6.3 Vitamin (A) deficiency			
1998	vitamin deficiency	维生素 缺乏	wéi shēng sù quē fá
1998	bioavailability of vitamins	维生素 生物利用度	wéi shēng sù shēng wù lì yòng dù
1998	absorption of vitamins	维生素 吸收	wéi shēng sù xī shōu
A.6.4 Iron deficiency or anaemia			
1998	iron deficiency	铁 缺乏	tiě quē fá
1998	iron bioavailability (in diet)	(食品中) 铁生物可利用性	(shí pǐn zhōng) tiě shēng wù kě lì yòng xìng
A.6.5 Other nutritional deficiencies			
1998	calcium balance	钙 平衡	gài píng héng
1998	acid-base balance	酸碱 平衡	suān jiǎn píng héng
1998	dietary mineral balance	膳食 矿物质 平衡	shàn shí kuàng wù zhì píng héng
1998	bioavailability	生物 利用度	shēng wù lì yòng dù
1998	bioavailability	生物 利用率	shēng wù lì yòng lǜ
1998	bioavailability of micronutrients	微量营养素 生物 利用率	wēi liàng yíng yǎng sù shēng wù lì yòng lǜ

by the World Health Organization between the 1990s and the early twenty-first century. This includes the study of lexical variations in the Chinese translation of original English nutrition terms, physical activities, food schema in nutrition research, sugar research terms, the use of adjectives in health research terms, public health research methodologies and nutrition recommendations. Lexical variations in health translation point to a long-existing issue in health translation: the readability and cultural appropriateness or efficacy of translated health resources, and the need to develop culturally adapted health resources to better engage the targeted audience, i.e. Chinese-speaking populations.

In specialised translation studies, there has been systematic research on textual, linguistic, discourse and stylistic differences between language for general purposes (LGP) and language for specific purposes (LSP) (Pietrzak, 2015; Baumann, 2007; Fischbach, 1998). Specialised translation of LSP differs from translation of LGP in terms of their communicative functions for the intended audience (Gerzymisch-Arbogast, 2007; House, 2008). While the translation of LGP tends to focus on the exact replication of information across languages, targeted translation of LSP is meant primarily to fulfil a social function.

The study of the translation, variation and assimilation of health terms is embedded within corpus translation studies, one of the most dynamic areas of applied translation studies. The specific translation phenomenon investigated is the wide co-existence of variant translations in public health. Variant translation is highlighted and defined as variant linguistic expressions, which tend to be picked up and used by translators or native speakers to indicate similar public health concepts and ideas in the source and the target health knowledge body and associated practices.

An important factor which underlines the establishment of particular translated terms among co-existing translation possibilities is the wide dissemination and social acceptance of translation materials by the target audience. The proliferation of variant translation remains a widely existent phenomenon in intensified cross-cultural and cross-lingual communication amidst the growing globalisation.

The variability of translation reflects the dynamics of the conceptual and language alignment between the source and target knowledge systems and societies. This study maintains that, different from earlier historical translation research, the availability of large-scale digital resources and associated corpus mining techniques and tools affords the systematic empirical data analysis of variant translation as collected in quantitative databases, with a view to developing new translation analytical models which are enhanced by advanced statistical analysis and corpus data modelling.

The integration of research methods from corpus translation studies as an emerging field in translation studies, and textual data mining and retrieval as a rapidly growing research field in information science, could help translators and academics to develop empirical measures and instruments to monitor and intervene in the selection and dissemination of specific types of variant translations. The integrated methodologies presented can be used to stimulate the growth of scientific concepts in the target language system by furnishing translators, researchers and the media with effective empirical tools in the purposeful production of translations, scientific research publications and media materials.

2 Exploring the latent structure of inter-sectoral communication of nutritional health in Chinese

2.1 Factor analysis of inter-sectoral communication of nutritional health: Global Chinese data

This chapter is divided into four sub-sections which illustrate the process that underlines the empirical corpus linguistic analysis of and comparison between the referential corpus, i.e. global Chinese language digital news database and the focus corpus containing news information published and circulated in mainland China. Firstly, Section 2.1 provides a statistical analysis of the patterns of the correlations between different industrial sectors in the communication of nutritional deficiency risks from 1998 to 2017. Because of the very large size of the global Chinese language dataset, it is first studied using exploratory factor analysis or principal component analysis to identify the latent factors in the database.

This leads to the construction of a statistical model with four conceptual scales revealing the strength of industries within each conceptual scale, as well as the relative distance between scales containing different sets of industrial sectors and types of businesses. Specifically, the four-dimensional model includes four sets of industrial sectors that may be broadly defined as 1) production and sales of food and beverages, 2) health research and services, 3) conventional transport (by air/railway/road) and sports, and 4) digital media and devices.

It is interesting to find out that some emerging and innovative industrial sectors are identified as integral parts in the last two dimensions. For example, e-commerce is included in the third dimension, and traditional Chinese medicine was attributed to the fourth dimension. These useful findings seem to suggest that in promoting and communicating the risks of nutritional deficiencies to specific cultural groups and communities, for example, the Chinese communities, established industrial sectors, emerging business models and traditional health practices could be leveraged – given the identified synergies of cross-sectoral interaction in the corpus analysis – to achieve enhanced outcomes of health promotion in national contexts.

As discussed in Chapter 1, the analysis of the global Chinese language digital database is to provide useful referential data and statistics for analysing and assessing intra- and inter-sectoral interaction, or the lack of it, in national contexts in terms of the communication of nutritional deficiency risks. Therefore, following the construction of the four-dimensional model with the global Chinese language dataset, a confirmatory factor analysis is conducted with the mainland Chinese dataset to test the applicability and suitability of the four-dimensional model extracted from the news information gathered from a much wider range of licensed and credible digital resources in the Chinese language.

The confirmatory factor analysis shows that while the first two scales of the general model built with the global Chinese dataset applied in the mainland Chinese dataset, the last two conceptual scales did not explain many of the variations in the patterns identified in the mainland Chinese digital news resources. This indicates the differences and dissimilarities between the two Chinese datasets under comparison which will be explored in Chapter 3 from the perspective of the cross-cultural framing and communication of nutritional health risks.

Section 2.2 builds on the corpus findings presented in Section 2.1 to explore the central question of who promotes what. As part of the result of the principal component analysis, lexical items in the Chinese keyword search index have been given their component loading scores across the four dimensional scales of the statistical model. When comparing the component loadings, relatively larger loading scores indicate stronger correlation between the lexical items and the conceptual extracted. By contrast, relatively smaller loading scores suggest weaker correlation between the Chinese health translation and the conceptual dimension built. Based on the assessment and comparison of the distribution of translated health terms across industrial sectors, Sections 2.2, 2.3 and 2.4 explore the connection between industrial sectors in the communication of specific nutritional deficiency risks in the global Chinese language dataset. This is followed by the same procedure in the analysis of the mainland Chinese dataset, particularly regarding the first two dimensions of the model, in an effort to address the question of who promotes what via the digital communication of nutritional health risks.

Table 2.1 provides the correlation among fifteen large industrial sectors. This is based on the correlation analysis of the global Chinese language dataset. The fifteen industrial sectors are Agriculture and Food Processing; Digital Devices; Beverage; Drugs and Pharmaceuticals; E-commerce; Economics; Food; Health Products and Services; Digital Media and Entertainment; Research; Restaurants/cafés/Fast Food Outlets; Retail; Sports; Traditional Chinese Medicine; and Transport (by air/

Table 2.1 Correlation matrix (Industry_All) (Significance, two-tailed)

	1	2	3	4	5	6	7	8	9	10	11	12	13	14	15
1	1.00	.152	.869	.583	.150	.759	.810	.638	.290	.312	.727	.234	.489	.340	.264
Sig	–	.261	.000	.004	.263	.000	.000	.001	.107	.091	.000	.161	.014	.071	.131
2	.152	1.00	.268	.130	.447	.398	.472	.368	.507	.502	.446	.287	.397	.602	.037
Sig	.261	–	.127	.293	.024	.041	.018	.055	.011	.012	.024	.110	.042	.002	.439
3	.869	.268	1.000	.497	.173	.741	.834	.649	.293	.384	.821	.386	.512	.516	.277
Sig	.000	.127	–	.013	.233	.000	.000	.001	.105	.047	.000	.046	.010	.010	.119
4	.583	.130	.497	1.000	.197	.797	.519	.796	.318	.748	.438	.340	.386	.383	.077
Sig	.004	.293	.013	–	.202	.000	.010	.000	.086	.000	.027	.071	.046	.048	.374
5	.150	.447	.173	.197	1.000	.419	.181	.426	.630	.358	.317	.361	.562	.347	.508
Sig	.263	.024	.233	.202	–	.033	.223	.031	.001	.060	.087	.059	.005	.067	.011
6	.759	.398	.741	.797	.419	1.000	.710	.856	.467	.772	.786	.401	.783	.558	.423
Sig	.000	.041	.000	.000	.033	–	.000	.000	.019	.000	.00	.040	.000	.005	.031
7	.810	.472	.834	.519	.181	.710	1.000	.597	.250	.482	.846	.473	.359	.661	.051
Sig	.000	.018	.000	.010	.223	.000	–	.003	.143	.016	.00	.018	.060	.001	.416
8	.638	.368	.649	.796	.426	.856	.597	1.000	.422	.754	.644	.278	.677	.657	.157
Sig	.001	.055	.001	.000	.031	.000	.003	–	.032	.000	.001	.117	.001	.001	.254
9	.290	.507	.293	.318	.630	.467	.250	.422	1.000	.415	.260	-.032	.459	.360	.238
Sig	.107	.011	.105	.086	.001	.019	.143	.032	–	.034	.134	.447	.021	.059	.156
10	.312	.502	.384	.748	.358	.772	.482	.754	.415	1.00	.554	.360	.505	.674	.070
Sig	.091	.012	.047	.000	.060	.000	.016	.000	.034	–	.006	.060	.012	.001	.384
11	.727	.446	.821	.438	.317	.786	.846	.644	.260	.554	1.00	.488	.619	.702	.258
Sig	.000	.024	.000	.027	.087	.000	.000	.001	.134	.006	–	.014	.002	.000	.136

(Continued)

Table 2.1 (Continued)

	1	2	3	4	5	6	7	8	9	10	11	12	13	14	15
12	.234	.287	.386	.340	.361	.401	.473	.278	-.032	.360	.488	1.000	.121	.376	.128
Sig	.161	.110	.046	.071	.059	.040	.018	.117	.447	.060	.014	–	.306	.051	.296
13	.489	.397	.512	.386	.562	.783	.359	.677	.459	.505	.619	.121	1.000	.403	.705
Sig	.014	.042	.010	.046	.005	.000	.060	.001	.021	.012	.002	.306	–	.039	.000
14	.340	.602	.516	.383	.347	.558	.661	.657	.360	.674	.702	.376	.403	1.000	-.164
Sig	.071	.002	.010	.048	.067	.005	.001	.001	.059	.001	.00	.051	.039	–	.245
15	.264	.037	.277	.077	.508	.423	.051	.157	.238	.070	.258	.128	.705	-.164	1.000
Sig	.131	.439	.119	.374	.011	.031	.416	.254	.156	.384	.136	.296	.000	.245	–

1 Agriculture and Food Processing; 2 Digital Devices; 3 Drink; 4 Drugs/Pharmaceuticals; 5 E-commerce; 6 Economics; 7 Food; 8 Health Products and Services; 9 Media and Entertainment; 10 Research; 11 Restaurant/Cafés/Fast Food Outlets; 12 Retail; 13 Sports; 14 Traditional Chinese Medicine; 15 Transport (air/road/water)

road/water). It should be noted that these industrial sectors are different from the original items of industrial and business classes provided by the Factiva database. Factiva's original classification scheme is more finely developed, containing tens of industrial types.

The fifteen industrial sectors listed in this study represent the aggregation of the original industrial categories in the Factiva database. For example, the category of Digital Devices includes businesses listed in the Factiva database such as those that sell orthopedic and physical therapy devices, mobile applications software, personal care products and appliances, personal electronics, portal software, smartphones, tablet computers, wearable technology, computers and consumer electronics and so on. Similarly, the category of Beverage includes businesses in the Factiva database: alcoholic beverages, non-alcoholic beverages, bottled water, brewing, Coke products, fruit juices, soft drinks, wine and functional beverages. The Food category investigated in this study encompasses original Factiva industrial classes: baby food, beekeeping and honey products, bread and other bakery products, breakfast cereals, condiments and sauces, confectionery, cookies, crackers and pasta, dairy products, food additives, food products, functional foods, starch, sugar, sugar substitutes, tobacco products, vegetable oils, ice cream and frozen desserts, and snack foods.

Typical examples of original Factiva businesses included in the health products and services category are oral care products, beauty/personal care, skin care products, soap and cleaning products, nursing and residential care, outpatient care, make-up products, biological therapy, cell therapy, child day care services, consumer goods, cosmetics and toiletries, dental care, facial care products, gene therapy, hair care products and hospital care. The Retail category used in the current study contains original Factiva industrial classes such as food retailing, supermarkets and grocery stores, warehousing and storage and wholesalers. The Sports category includes original Factiva businesses like footwear, leisure facilities, leisure and hospitality, sports equipment, and sports and physical recreation instruction. The traditional Chinese medicine category encompasses original Factiva industrial sectors: alternative health practitioners, herbal medicines and drugs, and traditional Chinese medicine. The Transport category contains more than a dozen original Factiva transport business subcategories: automotive, civil aircraft, commercial vehicles, highway, motor vehicles, transportation and logistics, urban mass transit systems, air transport, airlines, airports, alternative fuel vehicles, marine passenger transport, marine transport, passenger cars, railroad passenger transport and railroads.

This grouping practice is due to the fact that the corpus search results returned a mixed picture of the distribution of relevant Chinese translated health terms in the global Chinese language and mainland Chinese databases. While the frequencies of occurrence of the translated health terms are very high in certain industrial sectors, the frequency data in other industrial domains are not sufficient enough to enable a valid statistical analysis of the two databases under comparison. In the process of combing through original Factiva business types, only those which are largely similar to each other are grouped together and given a general industrial category. This has effectively solved the practical issue of limited or missing values in some of the original Factiva industrial domains, and led to a streamlined classificatory framework which includes only fifteen large industrial categories to be used later in the statistical modelling. With the mainland Chinese dataset, which is much smaller than the global Chinese digital dataset, further data enhancement techniques such as log transformation are used to enable the statistical modelling of the communication of nutritional deficiency risks across industrial sectors using typical parametrical tests such as multivariate and regression analysis.

Tables 2.2 and 2.3 provide the results of the exploratory factor analysis (EFA) of the global Chinese digital news data. EFA is a typical exploratory technique which helps identify the latent factors in the original dataset. The latent factors extracted by EFA often contain a number of the independent variables to maximally explain the detected variations in the dependent variable. In the current study, the original independent variables are the fifteen large industrial categories listed in Table 2.3. The EFA has extracted four latent factors from the original fifteen industrial sectors. The first latent factor contains five large industrial categories, which are Food, Drink/Beverage, Restaurant/Cafés/ast Food Outlets, Agriculture and Food Processing, and Retail. This is the latent factor which accounts for the largest amount of the total variance (26.73%) in the dependent variable, i.e. the distribution of translated health terms across the fifteen industrial categories in the global Chinese language database.

In Table 2.3, each industrial category has been assigned a component loading score. A component score ranges from 1 to -1. For positive values larger than zero, the larger the component score, the more important the contribution of the independent variable to the latent scale or factor extracted. For example, component scores larger than 0.6 often indicate strong correlation between the independent variable and the latent variable. By contrast, for negative values, the larger the component loading score, the less relevant the independent variable to the latent factor extracted by the EFA. For example, in Table 2.3, the largest negative component score is -.165, which was found between the independent variable Agriculture and Food Processing sector and the fourth latent factor associated with the last three industrial sectors in Table 2.3, i.e. Digital Devices, Traditional Chinese Medicine and Media and Entertainment. This statistical result suggests that

Table 2.2 PCA Model (total variance explained) (Industry_All)

Component	Initial eigenvalues			Extraction sums of squared loadings			Rotation sums of squared loadings		
	Total	% of variance	Cumulative %	Total	% of variance	Cumulative %	Total	% of variance	Cumulative %
1	7.66	51.102	51.102	7.665	51.102	51.102	4.010	26.733	26.733
2	1.91	12.737	63.839	1.911	12.737	63.839	3.442	22.946	49.679
3	1.59	10.615	74.454	1.592	10.615	74.454	2.457	16.382	66.061
4	1.17	7.822	82.277	1.173	7.822	82.277	2.432	16.216	82.277

Table 2.3 Rotated component matrix (Industry_All)

Variables	Component			
	1	*2*	*3*	*4*
Food	.863	.308	-.027	.254
Beverage	.851	.328	.211	.018
Restaurants/Cafés/Fast Food Outlets	.826	.282	.202	.297
Agriculture and Food Processing	.771	.427	.241	−.165
Retail	.574	−.053	−.005	.385
Drugs/Pharmaceuticals	.295	.878	.036	−.005
Health Products and Services	.389	.796	.208	.236
Research	.192	.762	.045	.469
Economics	.550	.687	.396	.177
Transport	.153	−.052	.935	−.116
Sports	.286	.405	.749	.198
E-commerce	.014	.115	.659	.591
Digital Devices	.208	.110	.111	.837
Traditional Chinese Medicine	.448	.396	−.136	.673
Media and Entertainment	−.083	.412	.458	.490

Extraction method: principal component analysis. Rotation method: Varimax with Kaiser normalization.

the Agriculture and Food Processing industry is minimally related with the fourth latent factor characterised by the use of digital devices and media in the communication of nutritional deficiency risks as reflected in the global Chinese language digital dataset. Within the first latent factor, the component loading score for the Food sector is .863, for Beverage it is 0.851, and for Restaurants/Cafés/Fast Food Outlets is 0.826. To a lesser extent, the component scores are 0.771 for the Agriculture and Food Processing industrial category, and 0.574 for Retail.

Table 2.2 shows that the second latent factor extracted by the EFA accounts for 22.946% of the total variance in the global Chinese language dataset. As a result, the combined variance accounted by the first two latent factors is nearly half of the total variation in the entire dataset, which in turn indicates the significance of the first two factors in the four-dimensional EFA model constructed. In Table 2.3, the second latent factor includes another four general industrial categories, which are Drugs and Pharmaceuticals, Health Products and Services, and Research and Economics. All four industrial categories contribute significantly to the second latent factor, as they all have large component loadings (larger than or close to 0.7) on the second dimension of the model: Drugs and Pharmaceuticals (0.878), Health Products and Services (0.796), Research (0.762) and Economics (0.687).

Similar to the first latent component, the links among these four industrial sectors are relatively easy to detect, as all of them have a strong focus on research-based business development.

The third latent factor extracted by the EFA, as Table 2.2 displays, accounts for 16.382% of the total variance in the entire database. This factor comprises three large industrial categories, which are Transport, Sports and E-commerce. The strength of this factor is indicated by the large component loading scores of these industrial domains on the third factor or scale: 0.935 (Transport), 0.749 (Sports) and 0.659 (E-commerce). The commonality among these three industrial sectors may be described as the transportation of objects and the movements of humans. It is very interesting to discover that E-commerce has been attributed to the third latent factor instead of the second latent factor, which contains industrial sectors such as economics. This corpus-driven finding seems to suggest that there is a growing synergy in the communication of nutritional health risks among these three industrial sectors representing conventional and innovative business models in transportation. However, this corpus finding is uncovered in the analysis of the global Chinese language dataset and its validity at the national level is yet to be tested with country-specific datasets.

The last latent factor extracted by the EFA explains another 16.216% of the total variance in the global Chinese-language digital media database. In total, the four dimensional models successfully explain as large as 82.3% of the total variance in the global Chinese digital news database. Three general industrial categories have been allocated to this factor: Digital Devices, Traditional Chinese Medicine and Media and Entertainment. The component loading scores for these industrial categories on the fourth scale are 0.837 (Digital Devices), 0.673 (Traditional Chinese Medicine) and Media and Entertainment (0.490) respectively. Similar to the third latent factor, the fourth factor as part of the EFA model has brought new and interesting insights into the cross-sectoral communication of nutritional health deficiency risks in the global Chinese digital database. For example, the corpus finding suggests that the distribution patterns of translated health terms display important similarities between businesses in the Digital Devices category and those in the Traditional Chinese Medicine category.

2.2 Confirmatory factor analysis of inter-sectoral communication of nutritional health: Chinese data

In order to test the empirical corpus findings that emerged in the study of the global Chinese-language dataset, this section will explore the mainland Chinese digital dataset by using confirmatory factor analysis (CFA) (SPSS Amos version 22) following the development of the four-scale instrument using the exploratory factor analysis (EFA). The function of CFA is to test the predictive power of the theoretical model constructed using the EFA. Specifically, this refers to the EFA model shown in Tables 2.2 and 2.3. The EFA contains four latent factors or scales with each factor or scale encompassing three to four major industrial categories. To verify and explore the validity of this four-scale model, which was built based on the global Chinese-language digital database, the CFA is applied in the analysis of the mainland Chinese digital set. The CFA can be used to produce scores indicating the statistical significance or the level of contribution of the fifteen industrial sectors to the four latent factors.

For example, in Table 2.4, three of the five industrial sectors remain highly correlated with the first latent factor: Agriculture and Food Processing, Drink and Food. The significance of their contribution to the first latent factor is indicated by asterisks in the column P (two-tailed at 0.05). This suggests that with the mainland Chinese dataset, the first latent factor largely remains valid with three important industrial sectors sustaining this scale.

Table 2.4 Confirmatory factor analysis (Industry_China)

Industrial sectors	Factor	Estimate	S.E.	P
Retail	F1	1		
Agriculture and Food Processing	F1	1.132	0.17	***
Restaurants/ Cafés/Fast Food Outlets	F1	0.155	0.14	0.268
Drink	F1	0.921	0.141	***
Food	F1	0.802	0.13	***
Economics	F2	1		
Research	F2	0.868	0.108	***
Health Products and Services.	F2	0.879	0.094	***
Drugs/ Pharmaceuticals	F2	0.819	0.123	***
E-commerce	F3	1		
Sports	F3	0.01	0.226	0.966
Transport	F3	0.008	0.192	0.966
Media and Entertainment	F4	1		
Traditional Chinese Medicine	F4	0.219	0.079	0.006
Digital Devices	F4	0.08	0.23	0.729

However, the other two industrial sectors, i.e. Retail and Restaurants/Cafés/ Fast Food Outlets do not seem to contribute significantly to the first latent factor as suggested by their significance values measured by P, i.e. larger than 0.05. Similarly, the results of the CFA show that the second latent factor extracted from the global Chinese language digital dataset remains valid for the mainland Chinese dataset. Three large industrial sectors still sustain the second scale, which are Research, Health Products and Services and Drugs and Pharmaceuticals.

Important differences begin to emerge when testing for the validity of the third and fourth latent factors extracted from the global Chinese-language digital news dataset. Specifically, the third scale does not appear to be relevant in explaining the variance in the dependent variable, i.e. the distribution of translated health terms in the mainland Chinese digital news dataset. By the same token, the fourth latent factor is weakly supported by the industrial sector of traditional Chinese medicine and thus indicates the unreliability of this scale when applying to the mainland Chinese data.

The question to be addressed at this stage is whether and to what extent the first two scales, which remain largely valid with the mainland Chinese digital news data, can explain variance detected in this dataset. Tables 2.5 and 2.6 demonstrate the results of the multiple regression analysis as part of the CFA. In the first regression model, the explanatory variables are defined as the valid components of the first latent factor, which are Agriculture and Food Processing, Drink and Food. Jointly they successfully explain as much as 87.221% of the total variance in the mainland Chinese dataset. In the second regression analysis model, the explanatory factors are set as valid components of the second latent factor as the CFA revealed. These are Research, Health Products and Services; Drugs/Pharmaceuticals. Similarly, this set of independent variables explains as much as 83.5% of the total variance in the mainland Chinese dataset.

Table 2.5 Multiple regression analysis: Model 1 (Industry_China Data)

Total variance explained

Component	Initial eigenvalues			Extraction sums of squared loadings		
	Total	*% of variance*	*Cumulative %*	*Total*	*% of variance*	*Cumulative %*
1	2.617	87.221	87.221	2.617	87.221	87.221
2	.234	7.803	95.023			
3	.149	4.977	100.000			

Extraction method: principal component analysis.
Agriculture and Food Processing; Drink and Food as explanatory factors

Table 2.6 Multiple regression analysis: Model 2 (Industry_China Data)

Total variance explained

Component	Initial eigenvalues			Extraction sums of squared loadings		
	Total	% of variance	Cumulative %	Total	% of variance	Cumulative %
1	2.505	83.514	83.514	2.505	83.514	83.514
2	.320	10.677	94.191			
3	.174	5.809	100.000			

Extraction method: principal component analysis.
Research; Health Products and Services; Drugs as explanatory factors

This interesting corpus finding demonstrates that either the first or the second set of the explanatory variables can independently describe and predict variations in the mainland Chinese digital news data. This may be explained by the fact that the global Chinese language digital news dataset encompasses a large variety of news sources from different Chinese-speaking countries and regions such as Hong Kong, Macau, Singapore and Taiwan, as well as Chinese-speaking communities living in multicultural and multilingual societies such as Malaysia, Australia, the United States and so on. The four-dimensional model built by the EFA also points to the distinct approaches to the communication and framing of non-communicable health risks, specifically nutritional deficiency risks, by different Chinese-speaking countries and societies at distinct stages of economic and social development. For example, the first latent factor contains five large industrial sectors which are strongly related to the agricultural processing, packaging and sales of food and drinks.

The relevance of this latent factor points to the significance of the Agriculture, Food, Beverage and Retail sectors to the communication of nutritional health risks and diseases. This has proved to be the case in this study. The validity of the second latent factor in the analysis of the mainland Chinese digital materials suggests that, apart from the significance of the agricultural and food industries, research-intensive industrial sectors such as Health Products and Services and Drugs/Pharmaceuticals also play a key role in the sectorally driven communication of nutritional health risks. As a result, these two sets of explanatory variables seem to characterise the mainland Chinese digital dataset constructed and analysed in the present study. It is envisaged that with different national datasets, this four-dimensional analytical model may at least remain partially valid, as this has been the case with the PRC data. The validity of the four-dimensional analytical instrument for the study of other national digital news corpora of similar structures will need to be tested in future research.

2.3 Who promotes what?

Following the construction and testing of the fourdimension EFA model, the next question is: given the proven similarities of industrial sectors within each of the four latent factors, what are the foci of their communication and framing of nutritional health risks? Answering this question can help advance understanding of what and how global health research findings and recommendations by international health authorities like the World Health Organization are selected, culturally adapted and communicated to local and non-English-speaking audiences by distinct industrial stakeholders and sectors operating in national settings. To explore this question, this section examines different sets of Chinese translated nutritional terms extracted from official Chinese translations of the WHO's global nutritional guidelines developed between the late 1990s and the early 2000s. The statistics discussed in this section, such as the factor loadings of translated health terms, form part of the exploratory factor analysis described in the previous section.

Table 2.7 lists seven health terms translated into Chinese which exhibit high loading scores on the first latent factor. The three translated Chinese terms which have the highest factor loadings are 热量 平衡 (rè liàng píng héng) (energy balance) (1.34218), 膳食 矿物质 平衡 (shàn shí kuàng wù zhì píng héng) (dietary mineral balance) (1.31461) and 维生素 缺乏 (wéi shēng sù quē fá) (vitamin deficiency) (1.02421). These are closely followed by 营养 均衡 (yíng yǎng jūn héng) (nutrition balance) (0.93468) and 均衡 饮食 (jūn héng yǐn shí) (balanced diet). The remaining two health translations with modest factor-loading scores are: 营养 利用 (yíng yǎng lì yòng) (nutrient availability)

Table 2.7 EFA Dimension 1 (Industry_Global Chinese Dataset)

Year	English term	Chinese translation (Pinyin)	Factor loading
1998	energy balance	热量 平衡 (rè liàng píng héng)	1.34218
1998	dietary mineral balance	膳食 矿物质 平衡 (shàn shí kuàng wù zhì píng héng)	1.31461
1998	vitamin deficiency	维生素 缺乏 (wéi shēng sù quē fá)	1.02421
1990	nutrition balance	营养 均衡 (yíng yǎng jūn héng)	0.93468
2003	balanced diet	均衡 饮食 (jūn héng yǐn shí)	0.79009
1998	nutrient availability	营养 利用 (yíng yǎng lì yòng)	0.68722
1998	nutrient absorption	营养 吸收 (yíng yǎng xī shōu)	0.57711

(0.68722) and 营养 吸收 (yíng yǎng xī shōu) (nutrient absorption) (0.57711). The large loadings of these health translations effectively point to the foci of communicating and prioritising nutritional health risks among the five large industrial sectors allocated to the first latent factor: Food, Drink, Restaurants/ Cafés /Fast Food Outlets, Agriculture and Food Processing and Retail.

The keywords that these five large industrial sectors have heavily invested upon are 'energy', 'minerals' and 'vitamins' (lack of sufficient energy in diets and deficiencies in minerals and vitamins). These reflect the industrial exploitation or selective utilisation of global health research findings in specific socio-economic and cultural contexts. In the same word list, keywords like 'nutrition balance' and 'balanced diet' seem to point to sectorally motivated approaches and solutions to the identified health risks posed to the specific populations and cultural groups under investigation, i.e. the global Chinese-speaking communities. Lastly, the two keywords with modest factor loadings, i.e. 'nutrient availability' and 'nutrient absorption', indicate a relatively minor sectoral focus of the culture-specific communication of nutritional risks.

Table 2.8 lists the eight translated health terms which have high or relatively large loadings on the second latent scale constructed by the EFA with the global Chinese language digital dataset. It is interesting to notice that translated health terms which are relatively lower loadings on the first latent factor, such as 营养 利用 (yíng yǎng lì yòng) (nutrient availability) and 营养 吸收 (yíng yǎng xī shōu) (nutrient absorption), are now listed as top keywords contributing significantly to the second latent factor. The top keyword on the list is 生物 利用率 (shēng wù lì yòng lǜ) (bioavailability), which represents a more abstract and complex health concept. However, this important corpus finding can be reasonably explained by the fact that industrial sectors attributed to the second latent factor are mostly typical research-intensive industrial and business categories such as Drugs and Pharmaceuticals, Health Products and Services and Research.

Table 2.8 EFA Dimension 2 (Industry_Global Chinese Dataset)

Year	English term	Chinese translation	Factor loading
1998	bioavailability	生物 利用率 (shēng wù lì yòng lǜ)	1.85444
1998	nutrient absorption	营养 吸收 (yíng yǎng xī shōu)	1.40095
1998	nutrient availability	营养 利用 (yíng yǎng lì yòng)	1.31369
1998	nutrition balance	营养 平衡 (yíng yǎng píng héng)	1.29464
1998	vitamin deficiency	维生素缺乏 (wéi shēng sù quē fá)	1.07057
1998	bioavailability	生物 利用度 (shēng wù lì yòng dù)	0.65396
1998	bioavailability of vitamins	维生素 生物 利用度 (wéi shēng sù shēng wù lì yòng dù)	0.51006
1998	energy balance	能量 平衡 (néng liàng píng héng)	0.49012

The two keywords which have large loadings on both the first and the second latent scales are 营养平衡 (yíng yǎng píng héng) (nutrition balance) and 维生素缺乏 (wéi shēng sù quē fá) (vitamin deficiency). This seems to indicate the potential areas of enhanced cross-sectoral interaction in the communication of nutritional health risks, despite the differences in the two sets of industrial sectors, i.e. the first set of industries with a strong focus on food processing and retailing and the second set of industries with a sectoral priority of health research. From the perspective of translation studies, it is interesting to notice how different sectors have developed their sector-specific usage of translated health terms, even when they are essentially referring to the same health research concepts.

For example, in Table 2.7, the Chinese translation of 'nutrition balance' is '营养均衡' (yíng yǎng jūn héng); in Appendix 1 the Chinese translation of the same English expression changes to '营养平衡' (yíng yǎng píng héng) which represents an interesting lexical variation of '营养均衡' (yíng yǎng jūn héng). Both '平衡' (píng héng) and '均衡' (jūn héng) indicate 'balance' in Mandarin Chinese, but the corpus finding suggests sectoral preference for specific usage of health terminology. For example, in Table 2.8, the Chinese translation of the English health term 'energy balance' is '能量平衡' (néng liàng píng héng). This seems to establish the preferred use of '平衡' (píng héng) over '均衡' (jūn héng) by research-intensive industrial sectors belonging to the second latent factor (for details of lexical variation in bilingual health translation, see the appendices).

Overall, the keywords listed in Table 2.8 exhibit a set of translated health terms which are more conceptually abstract and complex when compared with the keywords listed in Table 2.8. This can be explained by distinct approaches to the communication and management of nutritional health risks by industrial sectors belonging to the first and the second latent factors, respectively. That is, while the first sector, Food Processing and Retailing, invests in and exploits diet-based solutions to the identified health risks, the second sector, Health Research, focuses on tackling the health risks through advanced and innovative scientific health research for the targeted at-risk ethnic populations and communities.

Following the analysis of the distribution of translated Chinese health terms in the global Chinese language digital dataset, Tables 2.9 and 2.10 list and compare the use of Chinese health translations in the mainland Chinese dataset. The factor loadings in Tables 2.6 and 2.7 are part of the confirmatory factor analysis conducted with the mainland Chinese dataset. Similar to the exploratory factor analysis of the global Chinese digital data, in the interpretation of the CFA model, the larger the positive loadings, the stronger the correlation between the factor and the translated health term. The purpose of this section is to identify the top translated health terms in the

Table 2.9 CFA: factor loadings of translations (Industry_China)

Factor 1			Factor 2		
Explanatory variables:Agriculture and Food Processing; Drink; Food			Explanatory variables: Research; Health Products and Services; Pharmaceuticals		
Translation coding	English terms	Factor loadings	Translation coding	English terms	Factor loadings
T14 (TR)	dietary mineral balance	0.63859	T21 (TR/ SP)	nutrition balance	0.64676
T11 (SP)	vitamin deficiency	0.6702	T22 (TR)	nutrition balance	0.68444
T21 (TR/ SP)	nutrition balance	0.80702	T27 (SP)	nutrient absorption	0.83293
T12 (TR)	vitamin deficiency	0.87308	T12 (TR)	vitamin deficiency	0.99433
T27 (TR/ SP)	nutrient absorption	0.94025	T11 (SP)	vitamin deficiency	0.9987
T22 (TR)	nutrition balance	0.97388	T28 (TR)	nutrient absorption	1.11173
T28 (TR)	nutrient absorption	1.15033	T25 (SP)	nutrient availability	1.90884
T30 (SP)	bioavailability	1.27237	T26 (TR)	nutrient availability	2.06467
T25 (SP)	nutrient availability	1.58813	T30 (SP)	bioavailability	2.78908
T26 (TR)	nutrient availability	1.91846			

SP: simplified Chinese; TC: traditional Chinese

Table 2.10 CFA: factor loadings of translations (2) (Industry_China)

Year	Code	Chinese translation	Factor	Factor loading
1998	T26 (TR)	營養 利用 (yíng yǎng lì yòng)	F1 and F2	1.919
1998	T25 (SP)	营养 利用 (yíng yǎng lì yòng)	F1 and F2	1.588
1998	T30 (SP)	生物 利用率 (shēng wù lì yòng lǜ)	F1 and F2	1.272
1998	T28 (TR)	營養吸收 (yíng yǎng xī shōu)	F1 and F2	1.150
1998	T22 (TR)	營養 平衡 (yíng yǎng píng héng)	F1 and F2	0.974
1998	T27 (SP)	营养 吸收 (yíng yǎng xī shōu)	F1 and F2	0.940
1998	T12 (TR)	維生素 缺乏 (wéi shēng sù quē fá)	F1 and F2	0.873
1998	T21 (SP)	营养 平衡 (yíng yǎng píng héng)	F1 and F2	0.807
1998	T11 (SP)	维生素 缺乏 (wéi shēng sù quē fá)	F1 and F2	0.670
1998	T14 (TR)	膳食礦物質平衡 (shàn shí kuàng wù zhì píng héng)	F1	0.639

SP: simplified Chinese; TC: traditional Chinese

communication of nutritional deficiency risks by industrial sectors clustered into Factor 1 (Agriculture and Food Processing; Drink; Food); and those clustered into Factor 2 (Research; Health Products and Services; Drugs and Pharmaceuticals).

Statistics provided in Tables 2.9 and 2.10 point to important differences between the global Chinese-language digital news data and the mainland Chinese digital news data. In the global Chinese digital database, the two sets of keywords with large loadings on Factor 1 and Factor 2 exhibit distinct and contrastive patterns. It was found that industrial sectors belonging to Factor 1 (Food, Drink, Restaurants/Cafés /Fast Food Outlets, Agriculture and Food Processing and Retail) are strongly associated with words indicating lack of sufficient 'energy' in diets and deficiencies in 'minerals' and 'vitamins', and sectorally motivated solutions such as 'nutrition balance' and 'balanced diet'. By contrast, in the global Chinese dataset, industrial sectors as part of Factor 2 (Economics, Research, Health Products and Services; Drugs and Pharmaceuticals) are strongly associated with Chinese health translations representing more complex and abstract health research terms such as 'bioavailability', 'nutrient availability' and 'nutrient absorption'. This in turn reflects the distinct sectorally motivated prioritisation and communication of nutritional deficiency risks among the general public.

The translated health terms promoted by industrial sectors in the mainland Chinese data show very different patterns. In the mainland Chinese digital news data, the two sets of top translated terms which are strongly associated with industrial sectors in Factor 1 (Agriculture and Food Processing, Beverage, Food) and those included in Factor 2 (Research, Health Products and Services, Drug and Pharmaceuticals) are almost identical. The top three Chinese translations in both lists are 'nutrient availability', 'bioavailability' and 'nutrient absorption'. In the analysis of the global Chinese-language dataset, these three words have also been identified as top translations with strong association with industrial sectors belonging to Factor 2 (or the health research scale). This cross-corpus finding suggests very strong influence from research-intensive industrial sectors on the communication and prevention of nutritional deficiency risks among global Chinese-speaking communities and societies including mainland China.

More importantly, the corpus finding from the mainland Chinese digital corpus revealed that this influence has been limited to businesses and industrial sectors operating within the research-intensive industrial category, but also has largely extended to key Chinese industries specialising in the processing, packaging and retailing of food and beverage products. The significance of the influence is reflected in the two almost identical keyword lists which represent the focus of health communication – specifically, nutritional deficiency risks – by industries in the food processing and retailing scale and industries in the health research scale, respectively. This corpus finding points to important opportunities of developing and enhancing intra-sectoral and cross-sectoral cooperation and interaction around the communication of nutritional deficiency risks in mainland China, given the existing and growing synergies between the two large industrial classes, which are the agricultural processing and food retailing category and the health research category.

Statistics in Tables 2.9 and 2.10 also show that in both the global Chinese digital dataset and the mainland Chinese dataset, Chinese translations of 'nutrition balance' and 'vitamin deficiency' were detected as key items of health communication which have been promoted actively by industrial sectors across both scales, i.e. the agricultural processing and food retailing scale and the health research scale. This suggests another possible area in which cross-national and cross-sectoral cooperation could be explored and developed to tackle and manage nutritional deficiency risks among Chinese-speaking communities more effectively and efficiently beyond national borders.

Table 2.11 provide information about the key translations which are actively promoted and highlighted in digital resources from industrial sectors (Transport, Sports and E-commerce) belonging to Factor 3, which is part of the four dimension EFA model extracted from the global Chinese-language digital dataset. The list of keywords provided in Table 2.11 reveals important existing synergies in the cross-sectoral communication and framing of nutritional deficiency risks in the global Chinese dataset. Firstly, the two top health translation terms, 'energy balance' (factor loading: 1.990) and 'bioavailability' (factor loading: 1.619), were also highlighted in the communication of nutritional deficiency risks by industrial sectors belonging to the research-intensive scale (Factor 2 of the factor analysis model).

Table 2.11 EFA Dimension 3 (Industry_All)

Term no.	Year	English term	Chinese translation	Pinyin	Loading
T9	1998	energy balance	能量平衡	néng liàng píng héng	1.990
T17	1998	bioavailability	生物利用率	shēng wù lì yòng lǜ	1.619
T14	1998	nutrient availability	营养利用	yíng yǎng lì yòng	1.291
T2	2003	balanced diet	均衡饮食	jūn héng yǐn shí	0.824
T11	1990	nutrition balance	营养均衡	yíng yǎng jūn héng	0.740
T10	1998	energy balance	热量平衡	rè liàng píng héng	0.618
T20	1998	iron bioavailability (within diet)	(食品中) 铁生物可利用性	(shí pǐn zhōng) tiě shēng wù kě lì yòng xìng	0.547

Secondly, key health translation terms such as 'nutrient availability' (factor loading: 1.291), 'balanced diet' (factor loading: 0.824) and 'nutrition balance' (factor loading: 0.740) were identified as key items of health communication by important industrial sectors as part of the agricultural processing and food retailing scale (Factor 1 of the factor analysis model). The only item which has been identified as unique to Factor 3 (the transportation and sports scale) is the translation of 'iron bioavailability'.

Table 2.12 provides information about the key translations which are actively promoted and highlighted in digital resources from industrial sectors (Digital Devices, Traditional Chinese Medicine, Media and Entertainment) belonging to the Factor 4 (the media and digital innovation scale). Similar to the findings uncovered in Table 2.11, it was found in Table 2.12 that a number of health translations identified as keywords for Factor 4 are also top items in other factors. For instance, the Chinese translations of 'nutrient availability' (factor loading: 1.334), 'nutrition balance' (factor loading: 0.667), 'energy balance' (factor loading: 0.610), and 'balanced diet' (factor loading: 0.583) were also part of the keyword list for Factor 1 (the agricultural processing and food retailing scale). The translation of 'energy balance' was found as a key item not only for Factor 2 (the health research scale), but also for Factor 4 (the media and digital innovation scale).

The item identified as unique to Factor 4 is the translation of 'iodine deficiency'. However, when returning to the mainland Chinese digital news dataset to have a closer look at the distribution of the health translation of 'iodine deficiency', it was found that the statistically significant link established between this particular health translation and industrial sectors on the digital innovation scale is chiefly because of a large amount of Chinese media and news reporting of the health consequences of the Fukushima nuclear disasters in Japan in 2011. This resulted in a sudden surge of public concern, particularly in mainland China, about the purchase and consumption of foods with high iodine content like iodine-enriched salt and seafood

Table 2.12 EFA Dimension 4 (Industry_All)

Term code	Year	English term	Chinese translation	Pinyin	Loading
T9	1998	energy balance	能量平衡	néng liàng píng héng	1.694
T14	1998	nutrient availability	营养利用	yíng yǎng lì yòng	1.334
T11	1990	nutrition balance	营养均衡	yíng yǎng jūn héng	0.667
T13	1998	metabolic balance	代谢平衡	dài xiè píng héng	0.617
T10	1998	energy balance	热量平衡	rè liàng píng héng	0.610
T2	2003	balanced diet	均衡饮食	jūn héng yǐn shí	0.583
T6	1998	iodine deficiency	碘缺乏	diǎn quē fá	0.491

as a preventative measure to tackle the health risks posed by the looming nuclear pollution crisis. The following news excerpt was retrieved from mainland Chinese digital news data. It shows how iodine-enriched salt sold out quickly among the deeply concerned public following the disaster and the government's efforts to inform and pacify the public.

Title: 中国 提升 核 安全 信息 透明度 解除 民众 忧虑 (新华社 新闻) (22 March 2011)

过去 的 十多天 裹，日本 9 级 强震 引发 的 核电站 事故 一直 牵动 著 隔海相望 中国 民众 的 心。中国 环保 部门 迅速 启动了 辐射 应急 监测，并 提升 核 安全 信息 透明度。日本 强震 带来 的 核电 事故 仍然 为 不少 中国 民众 的 心理 蒙上了 一层 阴影，一些 城市 的 碘盐 甚至 遭到 抢购。

政府 一方面 迅速 增加 食盐 供应，卫生 专家 也 迅速 出面 平息 谣言。核专家 介绍，按 中国 目前 在 食盐中 添加 碘 的 水准，如 靠 碘盐 补碘 防 辐射，每天 摄入 的 食盐量 约 3 千克，早已 超过 人类 承受 的 极限，这种 做法 本身 十分 荒谬。同时，中国 国家 海洋局 多次 派出 船只 赴 黄海 取样，至今 未发现 辐射 异常。

Title: China increases the transparence of information on nuclear safety to pacify the public (Xinhua News)

In the past ten days or so, the nuclear plant accident following the 9.0-magnitude earthquake in Japan has been the focus of public concerns in China. Chinese environmental protection departments have reacted quickly to monitor the situation. This is to increase the transparency of information on nuclear safety. The recent strong earthquakes in Japan have caused Fukushima nuclear disaster. It remains a deep concern among the Chinese general public. In some cities, iodine-enriched salt has already been sold out.

On the one hand, the government has reacted quickly to increase the salt supply, on the other hand, health experts have urged to provide scientific information to the public to clarify confusion and dispel rumours. Nuclear experts comment that based on the current iodine level in salt consumed by Chinese families, one person would have to consume around three kilos of iodine-enriched salt per day to prevent the radioactive iodine-131. This would be far beyond the limit of human bodies and such behaviour is absurd. The Chinese State Oceanic Administration has sent various research ships to the Yellow Sea to examine the water samples there, but nothing unusual related to nuclear radiation has been detected so far.

Analysis in Chapter 2 up to this section has been based on a list of translated keywords (see Chapter 1 for the development of the bilingual health

Table 2.13 Global Chinese dataset – multiple regression model

Model summary[b]

Model	R	R Square	Adjusted R Square
1	1.000[a]	1.000	

a. Predictors: (Constant), Beverage industry
b. Dependent Variable: Ping Hang Shan Shi

search index) in the comparison between the two Chinese comparable corpora, i.e. the global Chinese digital new dataset and the Chinese digital
news dataset. The next section will examine the differences and similarities
between the two Chinese corpora with reference to specific translated nutrition terms. This is to identify industrial sectors at global and national level
(the PRC in this case) which can explain the maximum amount of variations
in the distribution of specific nutritional health terms in the two Chinese
digital media databases.

Tables 2.13 and 2.14 show the multiple regression analysis of the distribution of the two Chinese translations of balanced diet, i.e. 平衡膳食 (píng
héng shàn shí) and 均衡饮食 (jūn héng yǐn shí) in the global Chinese news
data and the Chinese news data, respectively. Important differences have
emerged in the cross-corpus comparison. In the global Chinese digital dataset, the most important explanatory factor is the Beverage industry, yet in
the Chinese digital resources, most of the variation in the past twenty years
in the use of 'balanced diet' can be explained by the Agricultural and Food
Processing industrial sector. This corpus finding seems to suggest that at the
level of global Chinese digital health communication, the Beverage industry
has driven much of the development of the health concept of 'balanced diet',
whereas in mainland China, the Agriculture and Food Processing industry, including the production of cooking oil, dairy products and meat and
poultry, seems to have the largest impact on the promotion of healthy diets
among the general public.

Tables 2.15 and 2.16 present the systematic differences between the
global Chinese digital data and the Chinese digital news data in terms of

Table 2.14 PRC Chinese dataset – multiple regression model

Model summary[c]

Model	R	R Square	Adjusted R Square
1	1.000[a]	1.000	1.000

a. Predictors: (Constant), Agriculture and Food Processing industry
c. Dependent Variable: Jun Heng Yin Shi

Table 2.15 Global Chinese dataset – multiple regression model

Model summary[b]			
Model	R	R Square	Adjusted R Square
1	1.000[a]	1.000	

a. Predictors: (Constant), Beverage industry
b. Dependent Variable: Ying Yang Jun Heng

the communication of the health concept of 'nutrition balance'. The two Chinese translations of the original English expression are 营养均衡 (yíng yǎng jūn héng) and 营养平衡 (yíng yǎng píng héng). Similar to Table 2.13, the industrial sector which explains most of the variation in the global Chinese digital news data is the Beverage industry. The finding presented in Table 2.16, however, differs from that in Table 2.14. The largest explanatory factor has been changed to the Restaurants/Cafés/Fast Food Outlets sector, which seems to have been playing a key role in the promotion of nutrition balance among the Chinese public. Chapter 3 provides detailed discussions on the role of the Restaurants/Cafés/Fast Food Outlets industry, including a range of Chinese, Asian and international fast food companies in the sectorally motivated promotion and communication of nutrition balance in the past twenty years in China. It was revealing to notice in these important corpus findings that industrial sectors such as fast food chain outlets and soft drink producers, which tend to be strongly associated with the development of chronic disease risks such as overweight and obesity, seem to have been key players since the publication of nutritional health research findings in the 1990s by global health research authorities.

The corpus analysis in this chapter analysed the distribution and use of health translations by different industrial sectors to promote and prevent nutritional deficiency risks. This is based on the comparison of two large-scale digital news databases: one is for global Chinese language digital data and one is for the mainland Chinese digital database. The use of exploratory

Table 2.16 PRC Chinese dataset – multiple regression model

Model summary[b]			
Model	R	R Square	Adjusted R Square
1	.990[a]	.980	.970

a. Predictors: (Constant), Restaurants/cafés/fast food outlets
b. Dependent Variable: Ying Yang Ping Heng

analyses constructed an analytical model with four latent factors or scales: first, the industrial category of agricultural processing and food retailing; second, the industrial category of health research; third, the industrial category of transportation and sports; and, lastly, the industrial category of media and digital innovation. This model was subsequently tested with the mainland Chinese data. The confirmatory analysis showed that while the first two scales held valid for the mainland Chinese information, the last two scales or factors did not seem to apply well in the case of the PRC. This model analysis streamlined the comparison of a very large number of original industries listed in Factiva in terms of the sectorally motivated communication of nutritional deficiency risks to the general public. The corpus analysis also identified important existing synergies among industrial sectors in the communication of health risks. The finding points to potential areas to further enhance and develop intra- and cross-sectoral cooperation and communication of nutritional deficiency risks and the sectoral approaches developed to tackle the identified health risks among the targeted populations and communities.

3 Patterns of inter-sectoral communication of nutritional health in China

3.1 Five new trends of cross-sectoral communication of nutritional health in China

As outlined in Chapter 1, the study of the global Chinese digital database is to provide the benchmark for the assessment of the PRC Chinese database. Table 2.1 provides the correlation matrix among fifteen large industrial sectors. This is based on the inter-sectoral similarity analysis of the global Chinese language dataset. The fifteen large industrial sectors under comparison are Agriculture and Food Processing; Digital Devices; Beverage; Medical Drug and Pharmaceuticals; E-commerce; Economics; Food; Health Products and Services; Digital Media and Entertainment; Research; Restaurant/Cafés/Fast Food Outlets; Retail; Sports; Traditional Chinese Medicine; and Transport (by air/road/water). Chapter 3 starts with a similar inter-sectoral analysis using the data collected from the mainland Chinese database (see Table 3.1). The inter-sectoral analysis explored the levels of similarity or the lack of it between the fifteen different industrial sectors listed above. The correlation matrix extracted from the mainland Chinese dataset was then benchmarked against the correlation matrix retrieved from the global Chinese dataset. This has led to the identification of systematic differences between the two datasets, i.e. the global Chinese dataset and the mainland Chinese dataset with regard to the strength of correlation between industrial sectors.

Specifically, five sets of important findings emerged from the cross-corpus comparison. These findings point to important trends in the growth of new business models of communicating and preventing nutritional deficiency risks among the targeted audiences in China. Firstly, in the correlation analysis of the Chinese digital dataset, important associations have been identified between the large industrial sector Transport and other four large industrial sectors: Food, Drink, Health Products and Services (particularly workplace health services) and Retail. The significance level of

Table 3.1 Correlation matrix (Industry_China) (two-tailed test)

	1	2	3	4	5	6	7	8	9	10	11	12	13	14	15
1	1.0	.308	.850	.739	.078	.575	.779	.623	-.189	.711	.057	.710	.391	-.034	.322
Sig	—	.036	.000	.000	.327	.000	.000	.000	.138	.000	.373	.000	.010	.424	.030
2	.308	1.0	.205	.245	.352	.309	.291	.391	.015	.055	.089	.282	.534	.125	.212
Sig	.036	—	.119	.078	.019	.035	.045	.010	.466	.377	.306	.050	.000	.237	.111
3	.85	.205	1.00	.576	.067	.554	.795	.541	-.046	.670	.045	.765	.145	-.056	.422
Sig	.000	.119	—	.000	.351	.000	.000	.000	.396	.000	.398	.000	.203	.374	.006
4	.739	.245	.576	1.00	.117	.696	.633	.817	.044	.691	.483	.439	.473	.095	.255
Sig	.000	.078	.000	—	.252	.000	.000	.000	.401	.000	.002	.004	.002	.294	.070
5	.078	.352	.067	.117	1.00	.395	.181	.376	.536	.154	.273	.183	.567	.279	.333
Sig	.327	.019	.351	.252	—	.009	.149	.013	.000	.188	.056	.146	.000	.052	.025
6	.575	.309	.554	.696	.395	1.000	.765	.859	.444	.813	.688	.637	.446	.331	.609
Sig	.000	.035	.000	.000	.009	—	.000	.000	.004	.000	.000	.000	.004	.026	.000
7	.779	.291	.795	.633	.181	.765	1.00	.624	.195	.675	.426	.741	.420	.196	.337
Sig	.000	.045	.000	.000	.149	.000	—	.000	.131	.000	.005	.000	.006	.129	.024
8	.623	.391	.541	.817	.376	.859	.624	1.00	.293	.748	.573	.530	.474	.209	.565
Sig	.000	.010	.000	.000	.013	.000	.000	—	.044	.000	.000	.001	.002	.114	.000
9	-.189	.015	-.046	.044	.536	.444	.195	.293	1.000	.185	.682	.032	.161	.470	.157
Sig	.138	.466	.396	.401	.000	.004	.131	.044	—	.144	.000	.428	.178	.002	.184
10	.711	.055	.670	.691	.154	.813	.675	.748	.185	1.000	.344	.561	.268	.126	.516
Sig	.000	.377	.000	.000	.188	.000	.000	.000	.144	—	.021	.000	.060	.236	.001

(Continued)

Table 3.1 (Continued)

	1	2	3	4	5	6	7	8	9	10	11	12	13	14	15
11	.057	.089	.045	.483	.273	.688	.426	.573	.682	.344	1.00	.101	.280	.462	.159
Sig	.373	.306	.398	.002	.056	.000	.005	.000	.000	.021	–	.282	.052	.003	.181
12	.710	.282	.765	.439	.183	.637	.741	.530	.032	.561	.101	1.00	.266	.064	.622
Sig	.000	.050	.000	.004	.146	.000	.000	.001	.428	.000	.282	–	.062	.358	.000
13	.391	.534	.145	.473	.567	.446	.420	.474	.161	.268	.280	.266	1.00	.142	.076
Sig	.010	.000	.203	.002	.000	.004	.006	.002	.178	.060	.052	.062	–	.208	.332
14	-.034	.125	-.056	.095	.279	.331	.196	.209	.470	.126	.462	.062	.142	1.00	.047
Sig	.424	.237	.374	.294	.052	.026	.129	.114	.002	.236	.003	.064	.208	–	.395
15	.322	.212	.422	.255	.333	.609	.337	.565	.157	.516	.159	.622	.076	.047	1.00
Sig	.030	.111	.006	.070	.025	.000	.024	.000	.184	.001	.181	.000	.332	.395	–

1 Agriculture and food processing; 2 Digital Devices; 3 Drink; 4 Drugs/Pharmaceuticals; 5 E-commerce; 6 Economics; 7 Food; 8 Health Products and Services; 9 Media and Entertainment; 10 Research; 11 Restaurant/Cafés/Fast food Outlets; 12 Retail; 13 Sports; 14 Traditional Chinese Medicine; 15 Transport (air/road/water)

the inter-sectoral correlation between Transport and the other four industrial sectors – Transport and Food; Transport and Beverage; Transport and Health Products and Service; and Transport and Retail – is well above the significance level of correlation attributed to the same industrial pairs in the global Chinese digital dataset.

This seems to suggest that as a major developing country, Transport (by air/railway/road) is playing an increasingly important role in the promotion of nutritional health through interactivity with other industrial sectors, particularly those which have direct access to and impact upon public health, such as Food, Drink and Retail. The detailed corpus linguistic analysis in this chapter revealed that this important cross-sectoral association established in the digital corpus analysis between Transport and the other four major industrial sectors in China was largely due to the rapid spread of traditional and, more importantly, innovative tourism forms, such as medical travel, health and wellness travel and senior or retirement travel which strongly drive the economic growth of tourism (coded as part of the Transport sector in this study), as well as other related industrial sectors in China.

Secondly, the inter-corpus comparison detected the more significant cross-sectoral interaction between the two large industrial sectors of Digital Devices and (workplace) Health Products and Services in the Chinese digital database. However, with the global Chinese digital news database, a statistically significant relationship between these two large industries did not seem to exist. Thirdly, the importance of digital industries was also reflected in the strong relationship between Media and Entertainment and Traditional Medicine, and Media and Entertainment and Restaurants and Fast Food. Fourthly, the comparison between the global Chinese digital news and the Chinese digital dataset pointed to an inter-sectoral association developing between Research and Retail.

These three sets of corpus findings reveal areas of growing inter-sectoral interaction and, more importantly, the great potential to innovate and transform traditional industrial sectors such as Traditional Medicine, Restaurants and Fast Food and Retail in the promotion and prevention of nutritional health risks through rapid technological and research development represented by Digital Devices and Research, as well as the instrumental role played by the Media and Entertainment industrial sector. Lastly, the cross-corpus analysis also identified growing interaction between Sports and Food at a level which is more significant than the sectoral information extracted from the global Chinese digital dataset.

Overall, the corpus findings seem to suggest a strong and growing trend of cross-sectoral interaction in the rapidly evolving health industry in China or the so-called big digitalised health industry in China (Wang, 2014; Wang, 2015). It benefits from the convenience of information sharing and utilisation brought about by research and digital technology advances. It is not only bridging the gap among traditionally divided industrial sectors such as Food; Beverage; Traditional Chinese Medicine, and Transport but is also giving rise to innovative cross-sectoral business models largely adapted to the targeted populations living in specific cultural and social environments – China in this case. The corpus finding also seems to suggest that these new innovative businesses born from the growing inter-sectoral interaction between traditional and digital or research-intensive industries are focusing on the growing social needs spurred by the changing demographic structure of the country – for example, a large retired or retiring population, and an increase in the middle-aged upper and middle class who are increasingly aware of and keen to invest in their health and well-being.

3.2   Inter-sectoral Interaction Between Transport and Food Industries

Table 3.2 provides statistics regarding the strength of correlation between the food industry and the other three industries. These three industries have been extracted for their detected significance of correlation when comparing the global Chinese digital news dataset and the PRC Chinese digital news dataset. It was found that while the food industry exhibited strong or statistically significant correlation with the sports industry and the transport industry in the PRC Chinese dataset, this was not observed in the global Chinese dataset. By contrast, whereas there is strong correlation between the food industry and the traditional Chinese medicine industry in the global Chinese dataset, such cross-sectoral association was not found with the PRC Chinese digital news dataset studied. In order to explore the inter-sectoral nature of the communication of nutritional health in the PRC Chinese dataset, we go

Table 3.2 Cross-industry correlation matrix: Food industry with other industries

Comparing global Chinese data with PRC Chinese data					
Industry	*Industry*	*Global Chinese data*		*China data*	
		P value	*Significance*	*P value*	*Significance*
Food	Sports	0.06	N	0.006	Y
	Traditional Chinese Medicine	0.001	Y	0.129	N
	Transport	0.416	N	0.024	Y

back to the digital news dataset to identify textual and linguistic patterns in the digital cross-sectoral resources and publications provided in the Factiva database. The following two examples were taken by using the search term '热量均衡' (rè liàng jūn héng) ('energy balance').

Title: 豪华 邮轮 一日五餐, 2013 年 6 月 18 日 《明报》

豪华 邮轮 设有 著名 星级 餐厅, 食物 水准 一流, 加上 24 小时 运作 的 客房 服务, 一不 留神, 随时 过分 搏命 吃到 滞。张总 谈到「初坐 邮轮时 感觉 新鲜, 即使 吃得 很饱, 仍 会 很想 吃 消夜 自助餐。近年 已 学懂 节制 来 确保 **热量均衡 (1)**, 有时 只 吃 汉堡包 作一餐。」「曾 两个月 内 连坐 两转 邮轮, 结果 共重了 4公斤, 回港 后 要 立刻 吃 菜汤 减肥。」他 指 近年 邮轮 公司 愈来愈 注重 健康, 部分 餐单 列明 菜式 **热量 (2)**, 让 乘客 吃得 更安心。

Title: Five meals a day on luxury cruises, *Ming Pao*, 18 June 2013

Luxury cruises are equipped with well-known Michelin-starred restaurants offering first-class foods. The twenty-four-hour food service on cruises makes it easier for the passengers to overeat. Mr Zhang recalled that when he travelled on a cruise for the first time, everything was very new to him. Even if he was very full after meals during the day, he would still like to have additional buffets at night. However, in recent years, he had learnt to restrict his diet to ensure *energy balance (1)*. Sometimes, he just had hamburgers as a meal. Once after two cruises in two months, he gained four kilos and was determined to eat only soup after he returned to Hong Kong. He also pointed out that in recent years, cruise companies have been paying more attention to health and some menus clearly list the *calories (2)* of foods so that customers can eat more health-consciously.

Title: 去 旅行 不肥 秘笈 2012 年 1 月 31日 《头条日报》

农历 新年 期间, 许多人 都会 趁 长假期 外游 一下。也有 不少 病人 覆诊时 体重 都 上升 了, 由 一至 两磅 到 十数磅 都有。从 观察 得出, 冬天 到 北美洲 或 欧洲 外游 的 人士 体重 升幅 较多, 原因 是 这些 国家 的 食物 份量 较大, 食物 脂肪 和 **热量 (1)** 亦高, 难以 保证 **热量 均衡 (2)**, 例如 汉堡包、薯条、意大利薄饼、芝士、肉肠、炸鱼 和 啤酒 等。同时 因 天气 冷 和 日短 夜长 的 关系, 多数 会 吃多 一点 来 保暖 和 减少 活动量。**热量 (3)** 消耗少, 吸收多, 当然 会 肥了 回来！

而 到 东南亚 国家、日本 或 台湾 的 人士 体重 升幅 较微 是 因为 食物 份量 和 口味 跟 中国的 差不多, 活动量 也 较高 如 去 酒店 泳池 游泳、到 海滩 参加 水上 活动 等。若 你 发现 今次 外游 完肥了，下次 要 做足 预防 措施，比如 自选 飞机餐－许多 航空 公司 都 会让 乘客 二十四 小时 前 选择 低脂 低胆固醇 餐、低卡路里 餐、水果餐、蔬菜餐 等，好让 你 在机上 也 可吃得 健康。选 低卡 饮品，特别 是 到 天气 较热的 地方，多选 清水、清茶、无糖 汽水、走甜 柠檬茶 等；避免过量 喝 啤酒、果汁、珍珠 奶茶、椰青、汽水、奶昔 等 **高热量 *(4)*** 饮品。

Title: Secrets to weight control while travelling, *Headline Daily*, 31 January 2012

During the Chinese New Year period, many people would like to travel overseas taking advantage of the long holiday. As a result, many patients learn they have gained weight during a health check after return, from one to two pounds to more than ten pounds. From observation, those who travel to North America and Europe gain the most weight because of the large portions of food served there which is ***high in calories (1)*** and fat such as hamburgers, potato chips, Italian pizza, cheese, sausages, fried fish and beer. This can make it difficult to keep ***energy balance (2)***. Because of the cold weather and short days, many travellers tend to eat more to keep warm and they reduce their physical activities. The reduction in the expenditure of ***energy (3)*** and high intake of energy results in weight gain.

By contrast, Chinese travellers to Southeast Asian countries such as Japan or Taiwan gain less weight. This is mainly due to the small portions of the foods, similar taste to Chinese foods and more physical activities such as swimming in hotels or participation in beach activities. If you find you have weight while travelling, it would be prudent to take more precautions on future trips. For example, self-chosen foods on the plane: many airlines allow their passengers to choose twenty-four hours before boarding low-calorie and low-cholesterol foods, fruit meals or vegetable meals to eat healthy while on board. Also, consider low-calorie drinks, especially when travelling to hot places. Choose water, tea or sugar-free fizzy water, or sugar-free lemon tea and avoid ***high-calorie drinks (4)*** such as beer, juices, pearl milk tea, coconut milk, fizzy water or milk shake, etc.

The two examples given above illustrate the cross-sectoral communication of the health research concept of 'energy balance' in the PRC Chinese dataset. Despite the different topics and contents of the two news stories taken from the PRC Chinese digital news database, they all point to an existing strong and growing association between the tourism industry (as part of the transport industry in the original data coding process) and the food industry in China. The two news stories highlight two scenarios in which nutritional health issues such as weight gain are particularly relevant to the rising middle class of Chinese who are exhibiting new tourism consumption patterns such as recreational cruising and overseas holiday travels during traditional Chinese festivals. In both news stories, an excessive amount of foods high in calories and fat was identified as the largest health risk factor among tourists travelling either by sea or by air. In the first article, the increase in energy intake was linked with a large variety of food options offered on cruises. In the second, the development of weight-related health risks among Chinese patients and holiday makers was due to lack of awareness of culturally distinct dietary patterns when they travelled overseas. The reporting thus pointed to two new and typical obesogenic environments which were created by the growing interaction between two large industries –food and recreational travelling – that are relevant in the current Chinese social, economic and cultural context.

3.3   Inter-sectoral interaction between Transport and Drink industries

Table 3.3 summaries the correlation analysis between the drink industry and another four large industries. The contrastive analysis between the global Chinese digital news dataset and the PRC Chinese dataset identified some useful patterns. Firstly, in the global Chinese digital data, the Drink industry was strongly associated with Sports, Traditional Chinese Medicine and Restaurants/Cafés/Fast Food Outlets. This, however, was not observed in the PRC Chinese dataset. The only statistically significant association was identified between the Drink industry and the Transport industry. It is suspected

Table 3.3 Cross-industry correlation matrix: Drink industry with other industries

Comparing global Chinese data with PRC Chinese data					
Industry	*Industry*	*Global Chinese data*		*China data*	
		P value	*Significance*	*P value*	*Significance*
Drink	Sports	0.01	Y	0.203	N
	Traditional Chinese Medicine	0.01	Y	0.374	N
	Restaurant/Cafés/ Fast Food	0	Y	0.398	N
	Transport	0.119	N	0.006	Y

that, similar to the strong association between the Food and the Transport industries observed in Table 3.2, this strong cross-sectoral correlation may be explained by the growing popularity of recreational tourism in China among its vast rising middle class.

In order to analyse insights into the digital data, we again go back to the PRC Chinese dataset collected from the Factiva digital news platform. The Mandarin Chinese translation of 'nutrition balance' '营养均衡' (yíng yǎng jūn héng) was used consistently as the search keyword.

Title: '云顶梦号' 崭新亚洲航程, 2017 年 4 月 19 日 《新明日报》

云顶 香港 豪华 游轮 品牌"星梦邮轮"旗下的 第一艘 邮轮"云顶 梦 号" (Genting Dream）将 在 今年 12 月 3 日 回到 新加坡，并 以 此 为 母港，展开 崭新 的 亚洲 航程。船上 35家 餐室 荟萃 世界 美食.丽星 邮轮 曾 荣获"舌尖上 的 游轮"美誉，这项 荣誉 再次 展现 在 "云顶梦"号。游轮 汇集 超过 35种 料理 风格，乘客 可以 一日 三餐 享用 环球 美食 风味。星梦 餐厅：全日 提供 丰富早、午、晚餐 家常 菜式，晚餐 时段 还 可 欣赏 精彩 LIVE节目。水晶 生活·健康 餐吧：供应 健康 轻食 和 新鲜 果汁，打造 **营养均衡** 的 饮食 体验。

Title: *Genting Dream* starts brand new Asian routes, *Shin Min Daily News* (19 April 2017)

The first cruise of *Genting Dream* of Genting Dream Hong Kong will be returning to Singapore on the 3rd of December 2017 and departing from Singapore to start a brand-new Asian route. Star Cruises was awarded 'Cruises on the tongue'. This will be displayed on *Genting Dream*. The food on the cruise embodies more than thirty-five cooking styles. Passengers can enjoy global food three times a day. The restaurant 'Star Dream' provides rich breakfast, lunch and home-style dinner accompanied by live shows. Café 'Crystal Life and Health' provides healthy light food and fresh juice to provide a new eating experience characterized by its ***nutrition balance.***

Title: 新航-新推养生膳食 2016 年 11 月 10 日 《香港经济日报》

航空 公司 季节性 换餐单，通常 都是 某 特定 地方 菜式，而 新加坡航空 却 玩 健康 主题 '美味 营养 系列'.新航 表示，此 构思 是 来自 乘客们 的 意见，认为 吃得 健康 为 时下 的 饮食 潮流，经 半年 的 研究，确可 在 航机上 实践。搭 飞机，大家 最怕 乾。为 解决 这 难题，这 中菜 餐单 中 加入了 汤水 及 甜品，利用 中药 食材 入馔，如 人参、杞子、雪耳，以 **营养均衡** 达致 健康。

Title: Singapore Airlines promoting new healthy diets, *Hong Kong Economic Times,* **10 November 2016**

Airlines change their menu according to the seasons and often provide local dishes. However, Singapore Airlines is now promoting a new health-themed menu known as the tasty and nutritious food series. According to Singapore Airlines, this idea was originally from its passengers who believe that healthy eating is the current food fashion. After research during half a year, it was determined that healthy eating was possible on airlines. What people are most afraid of is dryness (dehydration) when travelling by air. To solve this problem, the Chinese menu on the plane has added soup and sweets with ingredients from traditional Chinese medicine such as ginseng, goiji and *Tremella fuciformis* (snow mushrooms) to ensure **nutrition balance**.

The two examples given above illustrate the detected strong inter-sectoral correlation between the Drink industry and the Transport industry in the Chinese digital news dataset. The first news story was unfolded in the context of the promotion of recreational cruising. Different from the reporting of the negative health impact from on-board food options, this news story highlighted the health benefits of snacking (or 'light food' in Chinese), soft drinks and fresh juices to keep nutrition balance while travelling by sea. It seems that while there is a growing awareness among middle-class consumers of the health risks of foods high in calories and fat, this topic of health risks posed by sugary drinks has not been fully explored.

The second news story focusing on nutrition balance was framed in the context of travelling by air. It was reported that as a leading innovator of the transport industry, Singapore Airlines introduced new drink items to its menu to tackle dehydration among passengers on board. The airline company researched, conducted a trial and eventually updated its drink menu with new soups and desserts using traditional Chinese medicine ingredients and food materials to keep nutrition balance among the passengers. This was very successful, particularly among passengers with Chinese cultural heritage who appreciated the new culturally adapted drink menu. As we can see in these two excerpts, the nutritional benefits of beverages tend to be reported and framed more positively when compared with food options provided by transport and tourism companies.

In order to have a better understanding of the growing cross-sectoral interaction between the Beverage industry with the Transport industry (including tourism), an extensive search of companies in these two large industrial sectors was conducted to identify businesses that were actively involved in the communication and promotion of nutrition balance through beverage products in China. Table 3.4 lists some of the most-mentioned

Table 3.4 Most-mentioned companies in Drink and Transport industries: '营养均衡' (nutrition balance)

Companies	Country of origin	Products or services
Coca-Cola Company	USA	Soft drinks
PepsiCo Inc.	USA	Soft drinks
Air China Limited	PRC	Airline
McDonald's Corporation	USA	Fast food and soft drink
Cathay Pacific Airways Ltd	Hong Kong	Airline
Yang Ming Marine Transport Corporation	Taiwan	Ocean shipping
TransAsia Airways Corporation	Taiwan	Airline
China Huiyuan Juice Group Ltd	China	The largest privately owned juice producer in China
Hangzhou Wahaha Group Co. Ltd	China	The largest beverage producer in China
MTR Corporation Limited	Hong Kong	Subway
Nestle SA	Switzerland	Transnational food and drink company
Spring Airlines Co Ltd	China	Low-cost carrier based in Shanghai, China
Genting Hong Kong Limited	Hong Kong	Cruise and resort businesses
YUM! Brands Inc.	USA	Fast food
Yomeishu Seizo Co. Ltd	Japan	Traditional Japanese herbal liqueur
Asahi Group Holdings Ltd.	Japan	Beer and traditional liqueur
Besunyen Holdings Company	China	Therapeutic tea products and slimming medicines
Ctrip.com International Limited	China	Ticketing, package tour and corporate travel management
Mondelez International Inc.	USA	Confectionery, food and beverages
Hong Kong Dragon Airlines Ltd	Hong Kong	Airline
Emirates Airline	UAE	Airline
Evergreen Marine Corporation	Taiwan	Container transportation and shipping
Genting Singapore PLC	Singapore	Cruises
Hey-Song Corporation	Taiwan	Fruit drinks, tea and sports drinks
Ito En Ltd	Japan	Tea and soft drinks
Malaysian Airline System Berhad	Malaysia	Airline
Muntons plc	USA	Beer, wine and cider
Genting Malaysia Berhad	Malaysia	Cruises
Starbucks Corporation	USA	Coffee producer and coffeehouse chain
Singapore Airlines Limited	Singapore	Airline

companies in the Drink and Transport industries which have taken advantage of the cross-sectoral promotion and communication strategy; that is to say, to frame and sell their products and services in purposefully designed consumption environments which reflect the real-life settings and changing lifestyles of middle-class Chinese consumers, for example, overseas recreational tours, anniversary trips, business travel and daily commuting by rail, subway or private car. Such commercial promotion strategies are well-received by the target audiences, as such promotion strategies reflect the needs for healthy drinks to keep nutritional balance among the targeted populations.

3.4   Inter-sectoral interaction between Transport andHealth Products and Services industries

As explained above, a key component of the transport industry is tourism. Table 3.5 shows the strong correlation between another two large industries, the Health Products and Services industry and the Transport industry. This section takes a close look at the digital news data collected from the PRC Chinese dataset to identify relevant social and economic phenomena in China which has contributed to the statistically significant correlation between these two industrial sectors. In the extraction of news resources from the digital Chinese corpus, the Chinese translation of 'balanced diet' or 均衡饮食 ('jūn héng yǐn shí') was used consistently.

The following three examples demonstrate that the growing interaction between the two large industrial sectors, Health Products and Services and Transport (including Tourism) has given rise to a number of highly innovative social programmes and business models in the promotion of nutritional health among the targeted population groups. These include the design and construction of recreational villages as part of domestic touristic

Table 3.5 Cross-industry correlation matrix: Health Products and Services with other industries

Comparing global Chinese data with China data					
Industry	*Industry*	*Global Chinese data*		*China data*	
		P value	*Significance*	*P value*	*Significance*
Health Products & Services	Digital Devices	0.055	N	0.01	Y
	Retail	0.117	N	0.001	Y
	Transport	0.254	N	0	Y
	Traditional Chinese Medicine	0.001	Y	0.114	N

destinations for the large and growing retired and retiring populations in the Yangtze River Delta Economic Zone of China (example one); the combination of health and wellness travels with services such as seasonal spa and 'super-food' in five-star international hotel chains (example two), and the integration of nutritional diet, medical check and therapeutic treatment in increasingly popular medical travel programmes (example three). The three examples illustrate how traditional health services such as senior care (example one), convalescence (example two) and medical check and treatment (example three) have been increasingly and innovatively integrated into the growing recreational and wellness tourism business in China. In such a process, both domestic (example one) and international (example two and three) business innovators are playing a key role.

Example 1

Title: 旅游养老地产的开发模式之案例解读 2016 年 6 月 23 日中国新闻社

随着 社会的 发展，一些传统的观念 也在 不断地 变化，老年人 对下一代的 依赖性 在 减少，他们 越来越 倾向于 不和 子女 挤在 一起，而是 趁着 身体 健康 走出 户外. 一些人 选择 环境 好的 地方 或 适宜 养老的 方式 去 安享 晚年。加之 近几年 旅游业的 蓬勃 发展，老年 旅游团的 市场 份额 也 逐年 上升，极力 推动着 养老产业的 发展。绿地 ２１城·孝贤坊 位于 江苏 昆山 花桥镇 最东端，距离 上海市区 约４０分钟 车程，这个 高度 创新 的 项目 定位于 集 度假、尊老、国际商务 功能 于一身 的 新镇。开发商 在 整个 项目中 选出 一个 片区 配建 老年 住宅，除 提供 饮食、休闲、商业、娱乐、文化 等 基础 设施 外，还 提供 便于 老人 活动的 特色 设施。前来 居住的 大都是 长三角 区域 大城市的 离退休 老人. 孝贤坊 食堂 专门 聘请了 为老年人 进行 食谱 配制的 营养师，保证 老年人的 **均衡饮食**.

Title: A case study of new real estate development models to boost tourism for retired people, China News Service, 23 June 2016

With social development, traditional Chinese concepts are being changed. The elderly are becoming less dependent on the younger generations. They are getting increasingly inclined to live separately from their children and to enjoy the outdoor life when their health permits. Some of them choose places in a good environment or suitable for spending their retired life. With the rapid growth of the tourism industry, the market share of tourism for senior customers is increasing as well, which greatly promotes the development of the retirement living industry in China. Greenland City 21 (including the Filial Piety

Retirement Village) is located in the town of Huaqiao in Jiangsu Province. It can be reached from Shanghai by car in forty minutes. This highly innovative development project integrated various social functions into one project including vacation, respecting the elderly and international business. The developers selected a special area for building retirement village known as the Filial Piety Retirement Village. Most of the occupants are retired people from the Yangtze River Delta Economic Zone (an economic region in China encompassing Shanghai municipality, Jiangsu, Anhui and Zhejiang provinces). The community canteen invited a nutritionist to design the recipes for the elderly to ensure their *balanced diets.*

Example 2

Title: 瑞士酒店集团 推出 旅行 养生 及 应季 水疗 项目 2014 年 10 月 16 日 美通社

瑞士酒店集团 关注 客人的 健康 与 活力，将其 全球的 可持续 运营 扩展 至 顾客 层面，以 多种 新项目 帮助 客人 在 旅行期间 保持 健康 习惯。瑞士酒店 的 母公司 FRHI 酒店集团 的 水疗与健身 副总裁 Andrew Gibson 表示："旅行者愈发重视健康习惯的保持，事实上，一份 提交 给 全球 水疗 与 健康峰会 的 报告显示，'养生旅游'每年增长9%，比全球旅游业的整体 增长 快了 近 50%。"保持健康的 关键 要素 是 留意 *均衡 饮食 (1)*。旅行者 通常 要 克服 时差、消化不良、身体乏力 等 症状，瑞士酒店 汇总了 一些 有用的 建议，并 制成 图表，详细 列出 那些 能够 消除 这些 不适的"超级食物"，这些 及 其他"超级食物"被 世界各地 的 瑞士 酒店 厨师们 常规 采用，用于 打造 营养丰富的 *均衡饮食 (2)*。

Title: Swissotel promoting new programmes of health and wellness tourism and seasonal spa, PR Newswire, 16 October 2014

Swissotel focuses on the health and vitality of its customers. The Swiss hotel chain brings its global sustainable business operation to the customers and helps its customers to keep a healthy lifestyle through many new programmes. Andrew Gibson is the vice president of the spa and fitness section of the parent company of Swissotel, FRHI. He said that travellers were increasingly more concerned about maintaining a healthy lifestyle. In fact, in a report submitted to the Global Spa and Wellness Summit, it was highlighted that health and wellness tourism is increasing at 9% per annum, which is 50% faster than the global tourism industry. The key to a healthy life is *balanced diet (1).* Travellers normally have to overcome symptoms of jet lag, indigestion, and physical fatigue. Swissotel has gathered some useful suggestions and made a diagram which lists some 'superfoods' that may reduce such symptoms. These 'superfoods' are regularly used by chiefs of Swissotel around the world to create nutritious and ***balanced diets (2)***.

Example 3

Title: 《新.餐.厅》全台首家 医旅饭店餐厅 20 December 2014 工商时报

北投 健康 管理 医院 与 北投 老爷酒店 共同 打造的「台北 国际 医旅」今日 正式 开幕，结合 健检、医学 美容 与 温泉度假 的 此 一 全新 饭店，标榜 为 民众 提供「客制化 健康 及 美丽 的 乐活 假期」，并 希望 推广 健康 旅游 风尚。「台北国际医旅」设有 一诉 求纯正、纯洁的〈纯.PURE CUISINE〉餐厅.含在「一泊二食」度假 套装 中 的 晚餐 每客 订价2,200元，此 一 价位 不算 便宜，故 其 内容 为 何？「严选食材，讲究新鲜、原味」、「使用时令 蔬果及严选食材」、「专业营养师指导」，「强调 营养 封存 及 **均衡饮食**概念」，这些都是北投〈台北国际医旅〉馆内附设的〈纯.PURE CUISINE〉餐厅欲传达的理念。

Title: Opening of the first medical travel restaurant 'New Dining Hall' in Taiwan, *Commercial Times,* 20 December 2014

Beitou Health Management Hospital and Hotel Royal-Nikko have established the Taipei International Medical Travel programme. It integrates health check, medical beauty clinic and hot springs, aiming to provide customised health vacations to the public and to promote health and wellness tourism. As part of the Taipei International Medical Travel programme, it has a dedicated restaurant known as 'Pure Cuisine'. The dinner included in the two-day and one-night travel plan is priced at 2,200 NTD per person. This is not cheap, but why? The food served reflects and adheres to the principles of 'Pure Cuisine', which includes selecting the best materials to keep the freshness and original flavour of the food; using seasonal vegetables and fruits; instructions from professional nutritionists; and locking in the nutrients in the food for ***balanced diets.***

3.5   Inter-sectoral interaction between Transport and Retail industries

Table 3.6 compares the global Chinese digital database with the PRC Chinese digital dataset regarding the cross-sectoral correlation between the Retail industry and another six large industries: Agriculture and Food Processing, Drugs and Pharmaceuticals, Health Products and Services, Research, Restaurants/Cafés/Fast Food Outlets and Transportation. The correlation

Table 3.6 Cross-industry correlation matrix: Retail with other industries

Comparing global Chinese data with China data (significance at two-tailed)

Industry	Industry	Global Chinese data		China data	
		P value	Significance	P value	Significance
Retail	Agriculture and Food Processing	0.161	N	0	Y
	Drugs and Pharmaceuticals	0.071	N	0.004	Y
	Health Products and Services	0.117	N	0.001	Y
	Research	0.06	N	0	Y
	Restaurants/Cafés/Fast Food Outlets	0.014	Y	0.282	N
	Transport	0.297	N	0	Y

analysis shows that in the global Chinese dataset, while the strength of correlation between the Retail industry and Restaurants/Cafés/Fast Food Outlets was verified, the statistically significant cross-sectoral interaction was not found between Retail and the other five industrial sectors. By contrast, in the Chinese digital database, strong correlation (p value less than 0.05) was detected between Retail and the other five industrial sectors, including Transportation. In order to have insights into the cross-sectoral interaction between Retail and Transportation in the Chinese digital news dataset, we go back to the Factiva database using 营养均衡 'yíng yǎng jūn héng', or the Mandarin Chinese translation of 'nutrition balance' as the search keyword.

Examples 1 and 2 again point to the instrumental role played by tourism which drives the growing cross-sectoral interaction in the commercially orientated promotion of nutritional health by the Retail and Transport (including Tourism) industries. The first example is taken from the rapidly growing eco-tourism in the city of Zhalantun in Hulunbuir, Inner Mongolia, China. In this context, the retailing of 'green' food materials and processed foods by local growers was embedded in developing farm-based recreation (agri-tourism) in traditionally socio-economically disadvantaged regions of the country. In the second, the retailing of local fisheries' products, both fresh and processed or packaged, was revitalised by the development of cultural tourism, especially through the growth of folk festivals, in this case the traditional celebration of the beginning of a new fishing season in Yu Gan County in southwest China.

Example 3 is another important instance of the growing interaction between Retail (selling of packaged Chinese festival meals) and Transport (airplane food producers) industries. This has given rise to a new type of business: packaged airline meals designed for special occasions, particularly the Chinese New Year. This business model was developed and run by popular retailers such as the China Pacific Catering Services and TransAsia Catering Services which, apart from serving large airline companies, have adapted their products to communities and the public. Innovatively designed, their products were very well received for the quality and convenience of the food, and a growing general trust and interest in the health value of their foods using nutrition preservation technologies often seen on airlines.

Example 1

Title: 内蒙古扎兰屯市休闲农业加速乡村旅游, 2017 年 6 越 17 日 《美通社》

近年来，内蒙古 扎兰屯 市 党委政府 高度 重视 休闲 农业 观光 旅游 的 发展，充分 利用地理 区位、生态 资源、人文 资源、历史 文化、特色 产业 等 优势，将 休闲农业、现代农业、美丽乡村、生态文明 建设 融合 发展，着力 打造 扎兰屯市 休闲 农业 旅游 集散地。目前，金沃 生态 科技园 正在 对 园区 进行 提档 升级，加大 设施 农业 发展 力度，用 营养 丰富 的 富硒 水果、富硒 蔬菜，为 游客 提供 **营养均衡** 的 食材 和 加工 食品，打造 纯绿色 天然 食品 基地。今年 七月，园区 休闲 疗养 中心 将要 投入 营运，透过 聘请 专门 营养师，以 满足 不同 游客的 营养 需求。

Title: Leisure farming accelerates the development of village travel in Zhalantun, PR Newswire, 17 June 2017

Party officials of the city of Zhalantun in Hulunbuir, Inner Mongolia, China, prioritise the development of leisure agricultural tourism by taking full advantage of the strengths of the city in terms of its geographical location, ecological resources, cultural heritage, culture and history, specialty industries, etc. They are striving to convert the city of Zhulantun to a hub of leisure agricultural tourism in the province. Currently, Jin Ao Science and Technology Ecological Garden in Zhalantun is upgrading its services by investing in agricultural development, which includes, for example, growing selenium-enriched fruits and vegetables to provide ***nutrition-balanced*** food materials and processed foods to travellers and visitors. This is to develop a production base of natural and green foods. In this coming July, the leisure and convalescent care centre will come into operation. The centre will cater for the nutritional needs of customers under the guidance of professional nutritionists.

Example 2

Title: 余干：发展旅游注重接地气

2017 年5月15日 中国产经信息数据库

　　江西省余干县 积极 挖掘 传统 习俗，将 非物质 文化 打造 成 旅游 文化 品牌。在 康山 大堤 锣鼓山 码头，余干县 开渔节 期间 创造性 地 举行 隆重 复古 开渔 仪式。期间，余干 还在 锣鼓山 码头 举办了 美食 展示，"湖家妹"、"明祖湖"等 鄱阳湖 食品 品牌 企业，联合 余干县 农技协 的 水产 养殖户，将 **营养均衡**、包装 精美 的 深加工 鄱阳湖 产品，以及 野生 小龙虾、水蛭、黄鳝、莲子、莲藕 等 新鲜的 原生态 湖鲜，展示 给 开渔节 现场 来自 天南海北的 游人.

Title: Yu Gan (in Jiangxi Province, China): Development of tourism needs to have local flavour, 15 May 2017, China Industry Economics Services

Yu Gan County proactively explores its cultural traditions and creates quality tourism based on its cultural heritage. The county organised innovatively grand celebrations of the beginning of a fishing season at the harbour of Luo Gu Mount. The celebrations followed long-standing cultural traditions of the county. During the celebrations, there were also local food exhibitions. Many well-known food companies producing products from the Bo Yang Lake such as 'lakeside sisters', 'Ming Zu Lake' join hands with the agricultural technology association of Yun Gan County in the food exhibitions. They offer ***nutrition-balanced*** and well-packed products and other fresh foods from the Bo Yang Lake such as wild freshwater crayfish, leeches, swamp eel, lotus seeds to the visitors from across the country.

Example 3

Title: 最食安 中央厨房 空厨 年菜 选择多 华膳空厨 & 复兴空厨 2016 年 1 月 23 日 《工商时报》

华膳 空厨 是 市占 最高的 空中 厨房，有 30 多家 航空 公司 都是 华膳的 客房。曾任 观光 局长的 华膳 董事长 赖瑟珍 上任 后，积极 推动 华膳 多角化 经营，并自 2013 年 起 推出 年菜，获得 市场 颇 多 好评，且 年菜 销售 业绩 逐年 成长。由于「天上吃的」与「地上尝的」毕竟 不同，华膳 空厨 年菜 除了 都是 大厨 设计的「功夫菜」，另一个 特色 是：包装。有别于 一般 冷冻包 使用的 PE 塑胶袋，华膳 生产的 冷冻 食品 包装，均 采用 经 食品 卫生 检验 所 检验 通过的 高温 杀菌 铝箔袋，能够 有效 阻隔 水气、空气 与 细菌 入侵。消费者 可 将 冷冻 铝箔袋 直接 放入 水中 加热，不会 有 任何 有害 物质 溶出，完全 保持 食物 原汁原味 及 **营养均衡**.

Title: Safest central kitchen: Airline kitchen offering varieties of foods – China Pacific Catering Services and TransAsia Catering Services, *Commercial Times,* **23 January 2016**

China Pacific Catering Services has the largest market share which serves more than thirty airline companies. After taking office, the CEO of China Pacific Catering Services, Lan Sezhen, who was the director of the tourism bureau, has been actively developing the business portfolio of the company. Since 2013, China Pacific Catering Services has been offering new-year meals. This was well received and the company's sales have been on the rise. Since the meals served on the ground and in the air are different, the new-year meals offered by China Pacific Catering Services are designed by experienced chefs. These meals are also characterised by their packaging. Different from ordinary plastic bags, for they are frozen food products, China Pacific Catering Services uses foil bags which can effectively prevent the escape of water or air and contamination by bacteria. Customers may heat frozen foods directly in hot water with the foil bags to ensure the original taste of the food, as well as the ***balance of the nutrients*** of the food.

3.6 Inter-sectoral interaction between Digital Devices and Health Products and Services

Section 3.7 moves on to discuss another important trend of the growing cross-sectoral interaction among key industrial sectors in China. This highlights the role of technological advances brought about by digital innovation in the promotion and communication of healthy lifestyles and habits. Similar to previous sections, the detection of this particular trend which underscores the inter-sectoral nature of health communication in China was based on the comparison between the two large Chinese digital datasets under investigation, the global Chinese digital news and industrial information dataset and the PRC Chinese digital resources collected and coded from the original the Factiva database.

Table 3.7 shows the result of the correlation analysis between the two large comparable corpora. It was found that in the global Chinese digital dataset, strong correlation was founded between the Digital Devices industry and another four large industrial sectors: Media and Entertainment, Research, Restaurants/Cafés/Fast Food Outlets and Traditional Chinese Medicine. The only industry which has not developed a strong association with the Digital Devices industry was Health Products and Services with the p value (0.055) slightly above the threshold level at 0.05. However, this pattern was reversed with the PRC Chinese digital dataset analysis. That is, while the Digital Devices industry has developed a strong link (p value at 0.01) with the Health Products and Services industry, its interaction with

Table 3.7 Cross-industry e-correlation matrix: Digital Devices with other industries

Comparing global Chinese data with China data

Industry	Industry	Global Chinese data		China data	
		P value	Significance	P value	Significance
Digital Devices	Health Products and Services	0.055	N	0.01	Y
	Media and Entertainment	0.011	Y	0.466	N
	Research	0.012	Y	0.377	N
	Restaurant/Cafés/Fast Food	0.024	Y	0.306	N
	Traditional Chinese Medicine	0.002	Y	0.237	N

other industrial sectors remains largely underexplored, as shown by the low inter-sectoral correlation scores.

This revealing corpus finding seems to suggest that in the promotion and public communication of nutritional health, various cross-sectoral interaction models exist among the global Chinese-speaking countries and communities, and the Digital Devices industry is playing a key role in this process through its interaction with a range of industrial sectors, for example the detected correlation between the Media and Entertainment and Digital Devices industries (p value at 0.011), or the very strong cross-sectoral interaction between the Traditional Chinese Medicine and Digital Devices industries (p value at 0.002). However, in China, the cross-sectoral communication and promotion of nutritional health is chiefly built upon the detected alliance or association between the Health Products and Services and the Digital Devices industries. In order to understand this contrastive pattern, we go back to the Chinese digital resources database to explore social and economic events and phenomena which have contributed to the detected strong correlation between the Health Products and Services and the Digital Devices industries. In the analysis of the large-scale Chinese digital corpus, the Chinese translation of 'nutrition utilisation' or 营养利用 (yíng yǎng lì yòng) was used as the search keyword for illustration purposes.

Example 1

Title: 6成 上班族 关心 职场 健康

Subtitle: 透过「好在康健」平台和「瘦身动吃动」APP，康健人寿推广全方位健康观念

2017年4月27日 《工商时报》
康健 人寿「360°康健指数」最新 调查 结果 发现，60％ 的 上班族 (非 管理阶层 员工) 重视 企业 是否 提供 职场 健康 促进 计画，但 仅

27% 上班族 表示 公司 有 提供 相关 措施。而且 上班族 表示 自己 在 求职 以及 转职 时，都 会 考量 公司 是否 提供 职场 健康 计画。康健 人寿 总经理暨 执行长 邵骏崴 表示，康健 人寿 致力 推广 360°全方位 康健 生活，透过 数位 健康平台「好在康健」和「瘦身动吃动」手机APP，帮助 客户 ..... 寻求 外部 资源 如 心理 谘商、运动 指导、**营养利用** 和 饮食 等。康健 人寿 呼吁 民众 改变 日常生活 习惯，忙碌 上班族 可 利用「好在康健」会员 平台 随时 随地 管理 自身 健康。

Title: 60% of working class cares about workplace health: Cigna Health Insurance (Taiwan) promoting integral health through mobile apps, 27 April 2017, *Commercial Times*

The recent report 'Health Index 360' by Cigna Health Insurance (Taiwan) found that 60% of working class (i.e. non-managerial employees) cares about whether their companies provide workplace health-promoting programmes, although as little as 27% of working class confirmed that their companies have taken measures in this regard. Moreover, working-class people expressed that they took into consideration whether the recruiting companies provided workplace health promoting programmes when applying for positions. The General Manager and CEO of Cigna Health Insurance (Taiwan), Tim Shields, confirmed that his company is devoted to the promotion of workplace health programmes. Through digital health support platforms and applications such as 'Health with Cigna' and 'Weight Loss through Diet and Exercise', Cigna Health Insurance (Taiwan) is actively assisting its customers to identify external resources such as counselling, exercise guidance, ***nutrition utilisation*** and diets. Cigna Health Insurance urges the public to improve everyday life habits and busy working-class people can manage their health at any time through their membership with the 'Health with Cigna' app.

Example 2

Title: 智能手表 – 医疗互联网发展的助推器

2017 年5月11日 中国产经信息数据库

医疗 健康 系统 正在 经历 一场 随着 物联网 的 开端 而 产生 的 技术 繁荣。互联 设备 被 不断地 运用 到 医疗 领域 来 创造 新 的 解决 方案，同时 减少 支出。智慧 医疗 和 其他 相关 创新 被 定义 为 医生 和 病患 间 建立 数字化 的 连接，可以 为 病例 查询 提供 更 便捷 的 渠道，也 能 更 准确地 研究 病患 的 现状 和 历史 情况。智能 手表 是 个人身体 状况 的 指南针.这些 技术 能够 感应 你 的 生活 习惯，例如 吃饭、工作、睡觉 习惯，以及 用 准确 的 数据 分

析 人类 行为。你 可以 期待 从 智能 手表 获取 实时的 最佳 饮食 习惯 推荐 来 促进 你的 能量 水平 并 保持 健康。它 可以 学习 并 分析 你 身体 的 出汗量，当 你 应该 摄入 水 或 能量 饮料 时 推荐 合适的 摄入量 和 时间，来 让 你 时刻 保持 活力。一定 程度上，饮食 习惯 和 食物的 **营养利用** 也 可以 通过 先进 传感器 来 进行 研究。身体的 细微 状况 会 被发送 至 你 的 私人 医生,他 了解 你 的 完整 病例史 和 当下 生活 方式,因此 可以 非常 准确地 针对 你 的 患病 情况 推荐 药物。

Title: Smartwatch – accelerator of the development of medical internet, 11 May 2017, China Industry Economics Services

The health care system is undergoing rapid technological growth with the growth of the internet. In the medical domain, the internet facilitates new solutions while reducing costs. Smart health care and associated innovation is defined as the digital connection between doctors and patients. The internet provides more convenient channels for information seeking, and facilitates the study of patients' conditions and history of illness. Smartwatch is the compass to personal health. These technologies can collect data regarding your living habits such as eating, working and sleeping to enable the analysis of human behaviours using accurate data. You can expect to obtain real-time best dietary recommendations to increase your energy level and to stay healthy. Smartwatch can study and analyse the amount of your sweat. It can also make recommendations on the appropriate amount and time for drinking water or other energy drinks. To some extent, dietary habits and the ***nutrition utilisation*** of foods can also be studied with advanced sensors. Subtle changes in your health condition will be sent back to your personal doctor so that he can have access to your complete health history and your current life mode to make precise recommendations on prescription medicine.

Example 3

Title: 2016 年 值得关注 的 13 项穿戴式技术发展趋势

2016 年 11月 14 日 中国新闻社

Fitbit公司CEO James Park 最近 在 接受 《时代》 杂志 采访时 透露了 其 未来 产品线的 部分 细节 信息。'我们 肯定 会在 未来的 设备 当中 采用 更多 先进的 传感器 设计，从而 帮助 用户 在 提升当前 可 追踪 数据的 实际 精度的 同时，对 更多 细化 指标 加以 获取 及 审视，"Park 指出。"我 不能 说得 太 具体，但 人们 肯定 都 对 这种 可观的 发展 前景 感到 兴奋，包括 利用 此类设备 追踪 自己 的 血压、情绪 变化 乃至 更多 与 运动 成绩 相关 的 状

态 数据。我们 正在 致力于 实现 这 一切，并 将 成果 随时间 推移 逐步 发布。"一位 Fitbit 公司的 代表 还 指出，该 公司 正"着眼 于 各类 与 健康 及 保健 相关 的 重要 指标，包括 运动量、睡眠 以 及 **营养利用** – 并 将 这 一切 与 相关 慢性 疾病 (包括 糖尿病、心脏病 以及 肥胖 等) 联系 起来，考虑 如何 借此 帮助 全球用户 提高 生活 质量。"

Title: Thirteen trends of the development of wearable technologies, 14 November 2016, China News Agency

In a recent interview with the *Times*, the CEO of Fitbit, James Park, revealed some details of the future production line of the company. 'We will surely introduce more advanced sensing equipment in our future applications. This is to help our users to obtain and review more fine-tuned indexes while upgrading the accuracy of current traceable data', Park pointed out. 'I cannot go into too many details but people will definitely be very excited about this prospect which includes using this equipment to follow one's blood pressure, emotional changes and more exercise-related status data. We are striving to realise this and will be releasing these outcomes as time passes'. Another spokesman from Fitbit mentioned that his company is 'focusing on different kinds of important indicators related to health and health care such as amount of exercise, sleep and *nutrition utilisation*, as well as linking these with chronic diseases including diabetes, cardiovascular diseases and obesity and considering how to help global users to improve life quality'.

The three examples were chosen from the Chinese digital industrial resources database. They provide typical and useful examples of the growing interaction between the Digital Devices and the Health Products and Services industries in China. These examples point to three large areas of digital technology innovation that are directly linked with the Health Products and Services industry in China, especially for the purpose of promoting workplace health and well-being. These three areas are innovative and user-orientated mobile phone applications (Example 1), smart watch (Example 2) and activity trackers and wireless-enabled wearable technology devices that measure data such as the number of steps walked, heart rate, quality of sleep, steps climbed and other personal metrics such as dietary patterns and nutrition level (Example 3). In the first example, the American health insurance company Cigna developed and promoted two new mobile phone apps, 'Health with Cigna' and 'Weight Loss through Diet and Exercise', to actively assist its Chinese customers in seeking external resources based on their personal needs such as counselling, exercise guidance, nutrition and diets.

These culturally adapted mobile phone applications were particularly useful for working-class people whose busy routine often prevents them from receiving medical and health instructions through regular hospital and clinic consultation with doctors on maintaining healthy eating habits and an active lifestyle. Examples 2 and 3 illustrate and outline the growing business trend of major digital innovation companies such as Fitbit investing in the development and design of personal health devices and wearable products for the Chinese consumers. In fact, as the corpus analysis shows, this general trend is driven by not only large international digital companies but also a range of domestic digital innovation companies and health services providers such as private chain hospitals and health care products retailers. Table 3.8 provides the list of the most-mentioned companies and entities in

Table 3.8 Most-mentioned companies in Digital Devices and Health Products and Services industries

Companies	Country	Products or services
Apple Inc.	USA	Designs, develops, and sells consumer electronics, computer software and online services
Electronic Arts Inc.	USA	Video games on personal computers and mobiles
Alphabet Inc.	USA	American multinational conglomerate. It is the parent company of Google and several former Google subsidiaries.
Baidu Inc.	China	Chinese web services company
Beijing Xiaomi Technology Co. Ltd	China	A privately owned Chinese electronics company, also the world's fifth largest smartphone maker in 2015.Xiaomi designs, develops and sells smartphones, mobile apps, laptops and related consumer electronics.
Giant Wireless Technology Limited	Hong Kong	Develops, manufactures, trades and distributes telecommunication equipment
Hua Xia Healthcare Holdings Limited	China	Provision of general hospital services and pharmaceutical wholesaling and distribution
Harmonicare Medical Holdings Ltd.	China	Largest Chinese private chain of women and children's hospitals
HTC Corporation	Taiwan	Consumer electronics company designing and manufacturing devices such as mobile phones and tablets
LINE Corporation	South Korea	Japanese subsidiary of the Korean internet search giant Naver Corporation specialising in the development of mobile applications and Internet services
Salesforce.com Inc.	USA	Cloud computing company

the PRC Chinese digital database that are actively engaged in digital health innovation and the promotion of nutritional health through innovative digital devices and technologies.

3.7   Inter-sectoral interaction between Traditional Chinese Medicine and Media and Entertainment industries

This section analyses another important trend of the communication of nutritional health in China: the growing interaction between the Traditional Chinese Medicine and the Media & Entertainment industries. Table 3.9 lists the cross-sectoral correlation matrix between Traditional Chinese Medicine and other eight large industries, Digital Devices, Beverage, Drug and Pharmaceuticals, Food, Health Products and Services, Research, Media and Entertainment and Sports. These eight industrial sectors were highlighted for the statistically significant correlation between these industrial sectors and the Traditional Chinese Medicine industry in either the global Chinese dataset or the PRC Chinese digital industrial resources data.

Similar to previous sections, the level of inter-sectoral communication of nutritional health information was measured by Pearson's correlation scores computed for each industry pair. As Table 3.9 shows, it was found in the global Chinese data that the Traditional Chinese Medicine industry exhibited very strong correlation with seven of the eight industrial sectors. The only industry which had statistically insignificant inter-sectoral correlation with Traditional Chinese Medicine was Media and Entertainment (p value

Table 3.9 Cross-industry correlation matrix: Traditional Chinese Medicine with other industries

Comparing global Chinese data with China data (significance at two-tailed)

Industry	Industry	Global Chinese data		China data	
		P value	*Significance*	*P value*	*Significance*
Traditional Chinese Medicine	Digital Devices	0.002	Y	0.237	N
	Beverage	0.01	Y	0.374	N
	Drugs and Pharmaceuticals	0.048	Y	0.294	N
	Food	0.001	Y	0.129	N
	Health Products and Services	0.001	Y	0.114	N
	Research	0.001	Y	0.236	N
	Media and Entertainment	0.059	N	0.002	Y
	Sports	0.039	Y	0.208	N

at 0.059). However, this pattern was reversed with the PRC Chinese data. That is, the only industry which exhibited strong correlation with Traditional Chinese Medicine was Media and Entertainment (p value at 0.002); the rest of the eight industries were rather weakly associated with the Traditional Chinese Medicine sector.

Table 3.10 lists some of the most-mentioned companies in the Traditional Chinese Medicine and Media and Entertainment industries. They were highlighted in the Dow Jones Factiva database for the amount and relevance of the digital content published by these companies in the promotion of nutritional health in Mandarin Chinese. They were detected as key industrial players in the communication of nutritional health to the Chinese public, either through news reporting of new disease treatments benefiting from traditional Chinese medicine, or through the commercial promotion of personal health care products or nutrition supplements based on formulas or ingredients from traditional Chinese medicine. Table 3.10 presents a mix of both domestic and international, especially Asia-based companies that are pioneers in this regard. For example, whereas Shandong Dong-E E-Jiao (in northeast China) and Beijing Tong Ren Tang (founded in 1669) have been

Table 3.10 Most-mentioned companies in Traditional Chinese Medicine and Media and Entertainment industries

Company	Country of origin	Products or services
Eu Yan Sang International Limited	Singapore	Traditional Chinese medicine and natural health supplements: lingzhi, cordyceps, bird's nest, ginseng
British Broadcasting Corporation	UK	Broadcasting
Shiseido Co. Ltd	Japan	Personal health care products
Beijing Media Corporation Limited	China	Broadcasting
Cerebos Pacific Limited	Japan	Health supplements products
China Times Publishing Co.	Taiwan	Broadcasting
Oriental Press Group Ltd	Hong Kong	Broadcasting
Sanlih E-Television Co. Ltd	Taiwan	Broadcasting
Shandong Dong-E E-Jiao Co., Ltd	China	Traditional Chinese medicines, health care products
Singapore Cablevision	Singapore	Broadcasting
Tong Ren Tang Technologies Co Ltd	China	Largest producer of traditional Chinese medicine products
Youku Tudou Inc.	China	Online video sharing platform

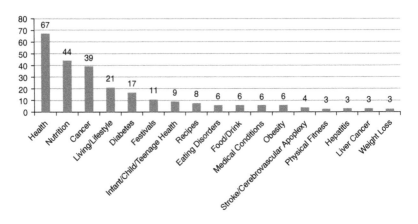

Figure 3.1 Top subjects covered by Traditional Chinese Medicine and Media and Entertainment industries

household names in mainland China for centuries and enjoy a high reputation among the older generations, the Singaporean multinational natural health products company Eu Yan Sang (or 余仁生) and the Japanese personal healthcare giant Shiseido (also known as 资生堂, zī shēng táng in Chinese) are gaining increasing popularity among the younger generations and middle-class Chinese.

Figure 3.1 lists some of the top subjects covered by the Traditional Chinese Medicine and Media industries. The statistics was extracted from the PRC Chinese digital database using the Chinese translation of 'nutrition absorption' 营养吸收 ('yíng yǎng xīshōu') as the corpus search word for illustration purposes. The two news examples given below were retrieved from the subject areas shown in Figure 3.1, Infant/Child/Teenage Health and Recipes, respectively.

Title: 肥胖儿童 的 推拿 护理, 2015 年 6 月 21 日 《文汇报》

推拿 疗法 有 治疗 范围 广、疗效 快、安全 可靠、简便 廉宜、易 于 接受 的 特点, 能 起到「未病先防, 有病可治」的 保健 及 治 疗 效果。对 肥胖 儿童 而言, 推拿 可 提升 他们 身体 的 各项 机体 功能, 对 神经、循环、消化、泌尿、免疫、内分泌 等 系统 的 生 理 功能 有 良好 的 调整 作用。蓝永豪 (香港 中医 学会 理事长) 表示 推拿 按穴 有助 促进 肝糖原 的 利用率, 还 可以 促进 核糖核 酸 的 合成, 提高 肥胖 儿童 机体 免疫力; 推拿 按穴 亦 有助 促 进 消化 系统 分泌 消化酶, 促进 小肠 **营养吸收**, 改善 新陈 代谢, 从而 调节 体重。

Title: Massage therapy for obese children, 21 June 2015, *Wen Wei Po*

Massage therapy can treat a variety of illnesses and is quick-acting, safe and reliable. It also has functions such as the prevention of illnesses and maintenance of health and well-being. For obese children, massage therapy can improve various body functions and regulate various body systems such as nerves, circulation, digestion, urinary, immune and endocrine. The chairman of the board of the Hong Kong Chinese Medicine Society, Yonghao Lan, explained that massage therapy could promote the bioavailability of liver glycogen and accelerate the synthesis of ribonucleic acid to improve the immune system of children. Massage can also increase the secretion of digestive enzymes to improve ***nutrition absorption*** by the small intestine and increase metabolism to enable weight loss.

Title: 冬日秘方 养生 五行 盛馔, 2014 年 11 月 13 日 星岛日报

踏入 冬季, **均衡 营养 (1)** 的 吸收 非常 重要。万豪 中菜厅 行政 总厨 叶国辉 师傅 参考 古代 医学 著作 《黄帝内经》, 藉 当中的 五行 概念, 创出「五行 滋味 宴」, 菜式 丰富, 烹调 方法 清淡, 让 客人 吃得 健康。叶国辉 师傅 五年前 到 内地 工作, 初尝 到 五行 菜式, 深 被 这些 以 不同 颜色 食材 制成的 健康 美馔 吸引, 并 启发 他 学习 医学 古籍 《黄帝内经》, 从而 设计 出 **营养均衡 (2)** 的「五行 滋味宴」。他 表示:「《黄帝内经》讲述 五行 概念, 包括 不同 颜色 食材 对 身体的 调理 作用。例如 代表 木的 绿色 食材, 能 强健 肝脏; 代表 火的 红色, 能 有效 护心; 属金的 白色, 可 帮助 润肺; 属 土的 黄色, 对 脾脏 有益; 黑色 食材 代表 五行中 的 水, 有利 补肾。五行 能 相生 相克, 以 这些 颜色 食材 入馔, 有助 **营养吸收 (3)**。」

Title: The secret to health and well-being in winter, 13 November 2014, *Sing Tao Daily*

In the winter season, it is very important to ensure ***nutrition balance (1)***. Chief Guohui Ye in the Chinese restaurant of Marriott created a new menu known as the Wu Xing or Five Elements Banquets. This is based on the traditional Chinese medicine classic Inner Canon of the Yellow Emperor or Esoteric Scripture of the Yellow Emperor. The menu is rich and the recipes focus on the freshness of the food. Chef Ye travelled to mainland China five years ago and first tasted so-called Wu Xing cuisine. He was deeply attracted to the cooking style of using food materials of different colours. This has inspired him to study the traditional Chinese medicine classic Inner Canon of the Yellow Emperor to create the ***nutrition-balanced (2)*** Wu Xing Banquets. He expressed that the classic text explained the concepts of the five elements: food materials of different colours have different regulating functions: green food materials can enhance functions of the liver; red food materials can protect the heart; white food materials can clean the lungs; yellow food materials are beneficial for the spleen; and black foods are good for the kidneys. Using these materials in cooking will enhance the **nutrition absorption (3)** from food.

3.8 Inter-sectoral interaction between Media and Entertainment and Restaurants and Fast Food industries

In order to understand the differences between the global Chinese dataset and the Chinese dataset, we go back to the large-scale digital publication database Factiva in an effort to identify Chinese or international companies belonging to the industrial sector of Restaurants/Cafés/Fast Food Outlets and Chinese media and entertainment sources which invest in the communication of health research related to nutritional deficiencies. These companies and media sources have contributed to the statistically significant correlation value which indicates strong cross-industry or cross-sectoral interaction between these two large industries in the PRC. The extraction of companies and media or news sources is based on the search for Chinese translations of nutritional health in the digital Chinese database. Specifically, the corpus search examined the distribution of the term 'Ying Yang Jun Heng', which is the Chinese translation of 'nutrition balance' in the Factiva database.

The search results show that the companies in the industry Restaurants/Cafés/Fast Food Outlets which promote heavily the concept of nutrition

Table 3.11 Cross-industry correlation matrix: Media and Entertainment and other industries

Comparing global Chinese data with China data					
Industry	*Industry*	*Global Chinese data*		*China data*	
		P value	Significance	P value	Significance
Media/ Entertainment	Digital Devices	0.011	Y	0.466	N
	Research	0.034	Y	0.144	N
	Restaurant/Cafés/ Fast food Outlets	0.134	N	0	Y
	Traditional Chinese Medicine	0.059	N	0.002	Y
	Sports	0.021	Y	0.178	N

balance ('Ying Yang Jun Heng') are a mix of both international and Chinese fast food companies. These include international fast food giants promoting typical Western fast food, such as McDonald's, YUM!, Kentucky Fried Chicken (KFC), Mos Food, Pizza Express, Pret A Manger, and beverages, such as Pepsi and Starbucks. The list also features vastly popular and household names selling and promoting oriental-style fast food in China, for example Ryohin Keikaku, better known as Muji (or 無印良品 ''wu yin liang pin in Chinese), a popular Japanese retail company selling a large variety of household and consumer goods including packaged snacks, seasonings and Asian fast food like instant noodles and microwave rice.

Compared with Ryohin Keikaku, which is more popular among younger generations in China, Aijinomoto or (味の素), the Japanese food and chemical company which produces and sells seasonings, cooking oils, sweeteners and amino acids, has been a household name for over four decades in mainland China. The company's product monosodium L-glutamate (known as MSG) forms an important part of many Chinese families' everyday cooking since the 1980s. Despite the increasing debates over its safety, it is still widely used in Chinese restaurants and eateries to enhance the flavour of the food.

The list in Table 3.12 indicates the growing competition from Asian fast food companies in Singapore, Taiwan and Hong Kong which design and sell

Table 3.12 Most-mentioned companies in Restaurant/Café/Fast Food industry promoting nutrition balance

Company	Country of origin	Products or services
McDonald's Corporation	USA	Fast food
Ryohin Keikaku Co. Ltd	Japan	Snacks
YUM! Brands Inc.	USA	Fast food
Inner Mongolia Yili Group	China	Dairy products
Starbucks Corporation	USA	Coffee
Wowprime Corporation	Taiwan	Oriental-style fast food
KFC Holdings	USA	Fast food
Mos Food Services Inc.	USA	Fast food
Cafe de Coral Holdings Ltd	Hong Kong	Oriental-style fast food
Ajinomoto Co. Inc.	Japan	Seasonings
BreadTalk Group Limited	Singapore	Bakery
PepsiCo Inc.	USA	Soft drink
Pizza Express Ltd.	USA	Fast food
Pret A Manger Ltd.	USA	Fast food
Xiwang Foodstuffs Co., Ltd	China	Corn oil
Sanquan Food Co. Ltd	China	Fast frozen food

Table 3.13 Top media sources reporting on '营养均衡' (yíng yǎng jūn héng) (nutrition balance)

Source	Chinese name	Publisher/Origin
China Economic News	经济时报	China News Service Ltd. (PRC)
Ming Pao	明報	Hong Kong
Beijing Cankao	参考消息	PRC
Oriental Daily News	東方日報	on.cc (Hong Kong) Limited
Sing Tao Daily News	星島日報	GC Media Teamwork Limited (HK)
Hong Kong Economic Times	香港經濟日報	Hong Kong Economic Times Ltd
Shanghai Securities News	上海证券报	Shanghai Stock Information Service Corporation
The Sun	太陽報	on.cc (Hong Kong) Limited
Apple Daily	蘋果日報	Apple Daily Limited
The Beijing News	新京报	PRC
Securities Times	证券时报	PRC
Wen Wei Po	文匯報	Hong Kong
East Week	東周報	GC Media Teamwork Limited (HK)
Headline Daily	頭條日報	GC Media Teamwork Limited (HK)

popular oriental-style fast food, from box lunches and noodles aimed at a working-class market to higher-end restaurant food that integrates Western, Japanese and local cooking techniques. These include Wowprime (known as 王品集团 or wang pin ji tuan in Chinese), a fast food restaurant chain from Taiwan which produces locally adapted versions of western and Japanese fast food and dishes targeting the growing middle class in China; Cafe de Coral (or 大家樂 or da jia le in Chinese, meaning 'the happiness of everyone'), a popular Chinese-style fast food chain from Hong Kong specialising in traditional Chinese breakfasts and afternoon tea; and BreadTalk (known as 面包物语 or miao bao wu yu in Chinese) from Singapore. Interestingly, the brand of a Singaporean bakery chain which is hugely popular among young people is based on the Chinese literal translations of a traditional Japanese literary genre 物语, or monogatari, which is broadly comparable to 'tales and legends' in English.

Lastly, the list also features popular Chinese fast food producers and retailers such as the Inner Mongolia Yili Group or 内蒙古伊利 (Nei Meng Gu Yi Li), specialising in dairy products like yogurt, infant formula, and a variety of milk products for adults; and Sanquan Food, known as 三全食品 (San Quan Shi Pin), which is the largest frozen food producer based in Henan Province in northwest China. The company produces and sells a wide range of Chinese frozen fast food like stuffed dumplings, steamed buns, rice cakes, microwave rice and traditional pastries that are frequently seen on the breakfast and lunch tables in many middle- and working-class Chinese families. The following two examples were extracted from the Chinese digital news data using the Chinese translation of 'nutrition balance' or 营养均衡 (yíng yǎng jūn héng) as the search keyword.

Title: 无印良品 开 餐厅 第一财经周刊 6 June 2017

你 以为 无印良品 只是 卖衣服的？不，它 是 开 杂货店 的，杂 到 连餐厅 都开。无印良品 将 淮海中路 旗舰店 三楼 的Café & Meal MUJI改成了MUJI Dinner（无印 良品 餐堂），它 一半 是 酒吧，一半 是 餐厅。这些 食物 要 达到「医食同源」的 标准，就是说，只选「对身体有益处的食材」。至于菜品 味道，用 无印良品（上海）商业 有限公司 的 总经理 山本直幸 的 话说，就是「以 较少 的 盐、糖、油 调味，把食材 最本身的 味道 带给 顾客」。「因为 中国 饮食 文化 渊源流长，并且 中国 一直 讲究 医食同源，在 **营养均衡**、以及饮食的 阴阳 方面 需要 采用 对 身体平衡 的 原则，这点 和无印良品 的 理念 非常 契合。」山本直幸 说，毕竟，能 接受 他们 所谓「健康饮食」以及「医食同源」概念 的 消费者 也 只有 亚洲 国家 了。

Title: Muji has opened a new restaurant, 6 June 2017, CBN Weekly

You may think that Muji only sells cloth. Now, it sells a variety of goods and has even opened a new restaurant. Recently, Muji has converted Café and Meal Muji on the third floor of the shopping mall located in Zhong Road, in Huaihai district, Shanghai. It has been converted to Muji Dinner, which is divided between a bar and a restaurant. Food served in Muji Dinner must reach the standard of 'optimal dietary and medicinal effect'. That is to say, Muji Dinner only chooses food materials that are beneficial to health. As for the taste of the dishes, the general manager, Yamamoto Naohide, said that they would bring the original flavor and taste of the food to the customers by using less salt, sugar and oil seasoning. China has a long tradition of food culture and has always focused on achieving the optimal dietary and medicinal effect of the food. The principles of traditional Chinese food culture such as ***nutrition balance*** and balance between Yin and Yang of the food for health balance match the principles of Muji very well. According to Yamamoto Naohide, customers in Asian countries can understand and appreciate the concepts of Muji such as healthy diet and the optimal dietary and medicinal effect of the food.

Title: 麦当劳 菜单 变 "少盐 好油 多果蔬" 19 July 2016 新京报

麦当劳 中国 首席 执行官 张家茵 在"麦麦全席"活动中 表示，麦当劳 将 带来 菜单上 的 三大 变革 – 更 少 盐、更 好 油、更多 蔬果 谷物，以 满足 中国 消费者 对 **营养均衡**(1) 膳食 日益 增长 的 需求。据 介绍，麦当劳 中国 自 2010年 至今，菜单 减盐 已 累计 超过 450吨，其中 汉堡面包、番茄酱 和 薯条 分别 减盐 10%、10% 和 20%。麦当劳 同时 计划 自2017年 起，将 全国 餐厅 的 棕榈油 逐步 替换为 营养 结构 更 合理 的 新配方 混合油，此外 还 将 陆续 推出 麦鲜粥、全麦 添加麦 满分、美味 鲜蔬杯、苹果片 等 多 种 **营养均衡**(2) 的 菜单。

Title: McDonald's has changed its menu to 'less salt, better oil and more vegetables and fruits', 19 July 2016, The Beijing News

The chief executive officer of McDonald's China, Jiayin Zhang, has indicated in a recent promotion activity that McDonald's will introduce three major changes to its menu, including using less salt, better oil and more vegetables and fruits, to cater for the growing demands from Chinese customers for *nutrition-balanced (1)* diets. According to some sources, since 2010, McDonald's China has reduced as much as 450 tonnes of salt in its food production, including ten per cent in hamburgers, ten per cent in tomato ketchup and twenty per cent in fried potato chips. It is planned that from 2017, McDonald's will change the current use of palm oil in its national stores to mixed oil with better nutritional value. It will also promote new dishes such as whole-meal porridge, vegetable soups and apple slices as part of a *nutrition-balanced (2)* menu.

3.9 Inter-sectoral interaction between Research and Retail industries

Table 3.14 compares the cross-sectoral correlation between Research and another seven large industrial sectors in the global Chinese and the PRC Chinese digital datasets. Again, important contrastive patterns were identified between the two large corpora. In the global Chinese dataset, the Research industry was consistently linked with new, digital or cultural health industries such as Digital Device, Media and Entertainment, Sports and Traditional Chinese Medicine. In the PRC Chinese dataset, however, the Research industry was strongly associated with primary and secondary industries like Agriculture and Food Processing, Retail and Transport. Such corpus findings seem to suggest that at the global level, health research findings tend to be more actively explored by new, digital or

Table 3.14 Cross-industry correlation matrix: Research and other industries

Comparing global Chinese data with China data (significance at two-tailed)

Industry	Industry	Global Chinese data		China data	
		P value	*Significance*	*P value*	*Significance*
Research	Agriculture and Food Processing	0.091	N	0	Y
	Digital Devices	0.012	Y	0.377	N
	Media and Entertainment	0.034	Y	0.144	N
	Retail	0.06	N	0	Y
	Sports	0.012	Y	0.06	N
	Traditional Chinese Medicine	0.001	Y	0.236	N
	Transport	0.384	N	0.001	Y

cultural health industries, while at the local level, such as the PRC, health research findings are being more actively utilised by primary and secondary industries.

Table 3.15 lists the Chinese and international companies and entities from the Research and Retail sectors identified as key industrial players in the promotion and communication of nutrition health in the Factiva database. The two examples given below help to illustrate how health and nutrition research findings are explored and utilised by retail companies in China. The first example is related to the explanation and reading of food nutrition labels for whole grain and sugar-free products, which caused considerable confusion among the public for a long period of time (Peng et al., 2012; Xu et al., 2014; Zhang et al., 2015). The second regards the development and distribution of new research-based nutrition tablets and food supplements by the Chinese internet café chain company with the largest number of internet café visitors.

Title: 警惕食品标签误导你

2015年12月21日, 中国新闻社

"全麦" 全麦 比 精制 粮食 含有 更多的 纤维素 和 维生素，但 市面上 的 全麦产品 并非 全部 都 由 全麦 制作。很多 商家 为了 满足 消费者 口感，多 选用 白面粉 制作，然后 加 少量 焦糖 色素 染成 褐色，但 其 **营养利用** 价值 远不及 真正的 全麦 面包。

"未添加 糖分"的 产品 并 不代表 没有 糖，所有的 食品，包括 水果、牛奶、麦片 和 蔬菜，本身 就 含有 糖分。因此，尽管 这些 商品 没有 额外 添加 糖分，原料 本身 也 可能 含有 糖分。

Table 3.15 Most-mentioned companies and entities in Research and Retail
industries

Company	Country of origin	Industry
FamilyMart UNY Holdings Co., Ltd	Japan	Retail
NTUC Fairprice Co-operative Ltd	Singapore	Retail
Shanghai New World Co. Ltd	China	Retail
Arcadia Biosciences Inc.	USA	Research
Chinese Academy of Sciences	China	Research
Columbia University	USA	Research
Hanwell Holdings Ltd	Singapore	Retail
Peking University	China	Research
A.S. Watson & Company, Limited	USA	Retail
Nanjing Central Emporium	China	Retail
Cerebos Pacific Limited	Japan	Retail
Taiwan Indigena Botanica Company Limited	Taiwan	Retail
Chengdu Hongqi Chain Company Limited	China	Retail
COFCO Limited (中粮)	China	Retail
By-Health Co., Ltd (汤臣倍健)	China	Retail
Grace's Marketplace	USA	Retail
Haoxiangni Jujube Co., Ltd	China	Retail
China Mengniu Dairy Co. Ltd	China	Retail
Red Mango, Inc.	USA	Retail
China Shengmu Organic Milk Ltd	China	Retail
Shenzhen Agricultural Products Co. Ltd	China	Retail
Uni-President China Holdings Limited	Taiwan	Retail
Want Want China Holdings Limited	China	Retail
World Health Organization	USA	Research
Walmart Stores, Inc.	USA	Retail
Whittards of Chelsea PLC	United Kingdom	Retail

Title: Warning of misleading food labels, 21 December 2015, China News Agency

The label of 'whole grain': Whole-grain bread has more fibre and vitamins than refined grains. However, not all of the whole grain products on the market currently are made of whole grains only. In order to create better taste, many producers tend to choose white flour in their production and then add some caramel pigment to change the colour.

The real *available nutrition* value of the products is thus far less than real whole-grain bread.

Title: 中国网吧集团开始通过 3 家网吧 试销 营养药

2014年3月13日 美国企业新闻通讯社

2014年3月11日，中国 领先的 连锁 网吧 中国 网吧 连锁 控股 集团, 简称 "CICC" 或"该公司" (OTCQB: CICC) 宣布, 该 公司 将于 未来 3个月 在 旗下 3家 网吧 门店 里 开始 试销 营养药 产品。这3家 网吧 分别是 Shijikuanxian、Shengpingfeiyang 和 Fuyan 网吧, 都 坐落在 广东省 深圳 龙岗区。3家 网吧的 平均 每天 访客数量 为 500人 左右。试销的 营养药 产品 包括 褪黑素片、维生素B 片、钙锌嚼片 和 复合 维生素片, 由 在 中国 专门 从事 **营养利用** 和 药物 产品 研发、生产 和 销售的 领先 生物 制药 公司 北京东方 协和 医药 生物 技术 有限 公司 (BEUB) 提供。

Title: China Internet Cafe Holdings Group starts trial of nutrition supplements in three internet Cafés, 13 March 2014, PR Newswire

On 13 March, 2014, China Internet Cafe Holdings Group (or CICC) announced that in the following three months, the company would conduct a trial of nutrition supplements in three of its internet cafes. These are Shijikuanxian, Shengpingfeiyang and Fuyan, which are all located in Long Gang district in Shenzhen, Guangdong Province. The average number of visitors to the three internet cafes is around five hundred people. The nutrition supplements on trial include melatonin tablets, vitamin B tablets, calcium and zinc chewable tablets and compound vitamin tablets. These are provided by a leading biomedical company, Beijing Oriental Union Medicine Biology Technology Co., Ltd, (BEUB) which specialises in the research of *nutrition utilisation* and the production and sale of medical products.

3.10 Inter-sectoral interaction between Sports and Food industries

Table 3.16 compares the inter-sectoral correlation between Sports and another seven industrial sectors: Beverage, Food, Media and Entertainment, Research, Restaurants/Cafés/Fast Food Outlets, Traditional Chinese Medicine and Transport. In the PRC Chinese dataset, strong correlation was identified between the Sports and Food industries. This stands in contrast with the global Chinese digital data analysis. The following example from the Factiva database illustrates how the Food industry as a traditional sector

Table 3.16 Cross-industry correlation matrix: Sports and other industries

Comparing global Chinese data with China data (significance at two-tailed)

Industry	Industry	Global Chinese data		China data	
		P value	Significance	P value	Significance
Sports	Beverage	0.01	Y	0.203	N
	Food	0.06	N	0.006	Y
	Media and Entertainment	0.021	Y	0.178	N
	Research	0.012	Y	0.06	N
	Restaurants/Cafés/Fast Food Outlets	0.002	Y	0.052	N
	Traditional Chinese Medicine	0.039	Y	0.208	N
	Transport	0	Y	0.332	N

is benefiting from its growing interaction with the emerging Sports industry. Similar to the corpus finding regarding the strong correlation between the Food industry and the increasingly popular health and cultural tourism industry (see Section 3.2, Inter-sectoral interaction between Transport and Food industries), new business models within the rapidly developing Sports industry such as public road running events are driving new waves of sectorally motivated promotion and communication of the benefits of energy balance and the absorption of nutrients through a more active lifestyle for the overall health and well-being of the public.

Title: 亚都丽致路跑住房 开拓 运动 旅客 市场 2015 年 5 月 22 日, 工商时报

台湾 每年 路跑 产值 高达 17 0亿元, 今年 路跑 赛事 场次 比 去年 翻倍 成长, 台湾 参与的 人数 也 大幅 增加, 不少 国际 路跑 选手 及 爱好者 也 常来 台 参与 盛事, 开启「运动 旅客」的 全新 市 场。亚都丽致 大饭店 自 去年底 积极 规画 专案, 与 日本 食品 大 厂 AJINOMOTO 海外 子公司 – 台湾 味之素 首度 独家 合作, 推出 「城市 路跑 乐. 从 亚都 出发」住房 专案, 提供 卓越 客房 5,799 元起的 优惠价, 并 搭配「AMINO VITAL」胺基酸 - 动 促进 **营养 吸收**, 及 提供 单趟 交通 接驳、翌日 延迟 至 下午2时 退房 等 贴 心 服务, 满足 跑者 或 运动 爱好者 需求。

Title: Landis Taipei invests in road running accommodation in the sports travel market, 22 May 2016, *Commerical Times*

The road running industry in Taiwan is worth as much as 170 million NTD a year. The number of road running events this year has doubled compared with last year. The number of both local and international participants has increased significantly, which has opened up a brand-new market in the sports travel industry. Landis Taipei since last year has actively engaged the Taiwanese subsidiary of the Japanese food company Ajinomoto in the planning of new hotel accommodation programmes. Landis Taipei will be promoting the programme of 'starting from Ya Du, enjoy running around the city', offering promotion prices of guest rooms for 5,799 NTD per night. This is matched by other services such as amino acid movement (or Amino Vital) to increase the *absorption of nutrition*, commuting services and late check-out at 2pm to cater for the needs of runners and sports fans.

4   Conclusion

This book studied and examined inter-sectoral interaction with a focus on Chinese-speaking societies. The study of inter-sectoral interaction around health communication was based on the construction and exploration of large-scale Chinese digital news corpora which contained large amounts of published and licensed industrial information and resources from global Chinese communities and especially the People's Republic of China over the past twenty years. In order to analyse the distinctive patterns between the global Chinese dataset and the PRC Chinese digital dataset, the researcher analysed the key public nutritional health policy documents and annual reports published by the World Health Organization between the 1990s and 2015, and extracted the Mandarin Chinese translations of the original English health terms.

It was found in the development of the bilingual health term index that lexical variation, instead of lexical consistency, widely exists in current bilingual Chinese–English health translation. A dozen types of lexical variation were identified in the comparison of the original English documents and their Chinese translations, including variations in the translation of nutrition balance, the bioavailability of nutrients, density of physical activities, sedentary lifestyle, culturally based dietary pattern research, food grouping schema, sugar research terms, use of adjectives in medical terms, health research methodology and nutrition recommendations (see appendices). The existence of lexical variation or inconsistency points to the lack of systematic research in the development of cross-lingual terminology for nutritional health. This also posed challenges for the compilation of the search term index for the study of the communication, commercialisation and promotion of health research findings in the Chinese digital industry news corpora.

To solve this problem, the researcher drew upon the classification of nutritional deficiency risks provided by the Global Burden of Disease (GBD) and identified the high-frequency Chinese translations of six classes of nutritional deficiency risks that are particularly relevant for the targeted populations. These are:

1   terms related to general nutritional deficiency risks and the mainte- nance of overall nutrition health;
2   protein-energy malnutrition and the balance of energy and metabolic balance;
3   iodine deficiency;
4   vitamin deficiency and the bioavailability and absorption of vitamins;
5   iron deficiency or anaemia and the bioavailability of iron;
6   other nutritional deficiencies such as calcium deficiency and balance, dietary mineral balance and the bioavailability of micronutrients.

In some of the nutrition health lexical categories listed above, valid vari- ant health translations were included in the translated health term index to ensure the systematicity and inclusiveness of the large-scale digital corpus search in Chinese.

The search for translated health terms in the two comparable corpora, i.e. the global Chinese digital dataset and the PRC Chinese digital dataset led to the extraction of a large number of industry reports and digital news related to nutritional health and the prevention of specific health risks. In order to streamline the analysis of the large amount of industrial information retrieved from the datasets, exploratory statistical analyses, including exploratory fac- tor analysis (EFA), were used to identify the association among different industrial sectors in the communication of nutritional health in Chinese at the international and national levels. This has led to the construction of a four-dimension EFA model which contains four analytical scales or factors. The first latent factor contains five large industrial categories: Food, Drink/ Beverage, Restaurant/Cafés/Fast Food Outlets, Agriculture and Food Pro- cessing and Retail. The second latent factor includes another four general industrial categories: Drugs and Pharmaceuticals, Health Products and Ser- vices, Research and Economics. The third latent factor comprises three large industrial categories: Transport, Sports and E-commerce. The last latent fac- tor extracted by the EFA contains another three large industrial sectors: Digi- tal Devices, Traditional Chinese Medicine and Media and Entertainment.

This four-dimensional model was then tested with the data collected from the PRC Chinese digital industry news corpus. It was found that while the first two factors of the factor analysis model remained valid for the PRC Chi- nese digital dataset, the third and fourth factors of the model required further testing and verification with more corpus data to be collected. This finding pointed out that important similarities and differences exist at national and international levels in terms of the inter-sectoral communication of nutritional health. Specifically, the similarities between the global Chinese and the PRC Chinese datasets are reflected in the strength and validity of the first and second factors or dimensions of the model. It suggests that with traditional primary, secondary and research-intensive industries, such as agricultural processing, food, drink, retail, drug research and pharmaceuticals, the modes and patterns of the communication of nutritional health in the global Chinese dataset and the PRC Chinese dataset have important overlaps. However, in new digital-based industries such as Digital Devices and Technologies and E-commerce, and cultural health industries such as Traditional Chinese Medicine and medical and health tourism (coded as part of the Transport industry), important differences need further exploration and analysis.

To understand the differences thus identified between the global Chinese and the PRC Chinese industry news data, Chapter 3 conducted a systematic comparison between the correlation scores and significance levels attributed to different industry pairs in the two comparable Chinese digital corpora. This led to the identification of important and growing trends of inter-sectoral communication of nutritional health in China, as in a number of cases, the strength of correlation between industries in the PRC Chinese dataset was identified as significant, in contrast with the lack of significance between these industrial pairs in the global Chinese industry news corpus. Chapter 3 analysed the inter-sectoral interaction between nine pairs of industries in the PRC Chinese dataset: Transport and Food; Transport and Drink; Transport and Health Products and Services; Transport and Retail; Digital Devices and Health Products and Services; Media and Entertainment and Traditional Medicine; Media and Entertainment and Restaurants and Fast Food; Research and Retail; and Sports and Food.

To illustrate these emerging patterns identified in the corpus analysis, relevant and typical industry news and media reports were retrieved from the digital corpora, which contain a wealth of real-life examples and social phenomena that exemplify these growing industrial trends and innovation patterns. It was found that despite limited research in this area, inter-sectoral interaction has driven and continues to underscore the development of innovative social programmes and projects and business initiatives that are transforming traditional and emerging digital-based industrial sectors. In this process, traditional industrial sectors such as transport (by air, road and rail), food and drink are benefitting from innovative tourism forms such as health, medical, cultural and retirement tourism; new digital health industries, especially mobile and wearable digital devices; and cultural health industries, for instance traditional medicine and therapeutic treatment. This study integrated methodologies from corpus linguistics, translation studies and digital media to analyse inter-sectoral interaction as an intervention tool. It highlighted benefits of developing and leveraging inter-sectoral interaction to provide effective, innovative and cost-effective approaches to the communication of nutrition health among the public.

Appendix 1
Translation of 'nutrition balance'

Date	Original English expression	Chinese translation	Pinyin annotation
1998	balanced diet	平衡膳食	píng héng shàn shí
2003	balanced diet	均衡饮食	jūn héng yǐn shí
1998	calcium balance	钙平衡	gài píng héng
1998	acid-base balance	酸碱平衡	suān jiǎn píng héng
1998	energy balance	能量平衡	néng liàng píng héng
1998	energy balance	热量平衡	rè néng píng héng
1990	nutrition balance	营养均衡	yíng yǎng jūn héng
1998	nutrition balance	营养平衡	yíng yǎng píng héng
1998	metabolic balance	代谢平衡	dàixiè píng héng

Appendix 2

Translation of 'bioavailability'

Date	Original English expression	Chinese translation	Pinyin annotation
1998	nutrient availability	营养利用	yíng yǎng lì yòng
1998	bioavailability	生物利用度	shēngwù lìyòng dù
1998	bioavailability	生物利用率	shēng wù lì yòng lǜ
1998	bioavailability of vitamins	维生素生物利用度 (维生素吸收)	hú luó bo sù sheng wù lì yòng dù
1998	bioavailability of micronutrients	微量营养素生物利用率 (微量元素吸收)	wéi liàng yíng yang sù sheng wù lì yòng lǜ
1998	iron bioavailability (within diet)	(食品中) 铁生物可利用性 (铁_吸收_营养)	(shípǐn zhōng) tiě shēngwù kě lì yòng xìng

Appendix 3

Translation of intensity of physical activities

Date	Original English expression	Chinese translation	Pinyin annotation
1998	activity	活性	Huóxìng
1990	inactivity	不活动	bù huódòng
1998	activity levels	活动量	huódòng liàng
1998	exercise	锻炼	Duànliàn
2003	exercise patterns	锻炼方式	duànliàn fāngshì
2003	lack of physical activity	缺乏体力活动	quēfá tǐlì huódòng
2003	moderate-intensity activity	中等强度活动	zhōngděng qiángdù huódòng
2003	30–60 minutes of moderate activity	30/60分钟中等强度活动	30/60 fēnzhōng zhōngděng qiángdù huódòng
1998	efficiency of physical activity	体力活动效率	tǐlì huódòng xiàolǜ

Note: Lexical variation in the translation of physical activities

Appendix 4

Translation of 'physical activity'

Date	Original English expression	Chinese translation	Pinyin annotation
1990	physical activity	体力劳动	tǐlì láodòng
1990	physical activity	体力活动	tǐlì huódòng
1998	physical activity	运动	Yùndòng
1998	physical activity	体力锻炼	tǐlì duànliàn
1998	physical activity	体育锻炼	tǐyù duànliàn
2003	physical activity	体力活动	tǐlì huódòng
1990	physical exercise	体力锻炼	tǐlì duànliàn
2003	physical fitness	体适能	tǐ shì néng
2003	physical inactivity	缺乏体力活动	quēfá tǐlì huódòng
1998	physical over-activity	超负荷体力活动	chāo fùhè tǐlì huódòng
2003	physically demanding manual tasks	体力劳动	tǐlì láodòng

Note: Lexical variation in the translation of physical activities

Appendix 5
Translation of 'sedentary lifestyle'

Date	Original English expression	Chinese translation	Pinyin annotation
1998	sedentary lifestyle	久坐不动的生活模式	jiǔ zuò bù dòng de shēnghuó móshì
2003	sedentary lifestyle	静坐生活方式	jìngzuò shēnghuó fāngshì
1990	sedentary life-style	久坐生活方式	jiǔ zuò shēnghuó fāngshì
2003	sedentary pattern	伏案工作	fú'àn gōngzuò
1998	social activities	生产活动	shēngchǎn huódòng
1998	sedentary individuals	安静个体	Ānjìng gètǐ
2003	obesogenic environment	易于肥胖环境	yìyú féipàng huánjìng
2003	passive overconsumption	被动过量消耗	bèidòng guòliàng xiāohào

Note: Lexical variation in the translation of physical activities

Appendix 6
Translation of culturally based dietary pattern research

Date	Original English expression	Chinese translation	Pinyin annotation
Foods translated as '食品' (shípǐn)			
1998	food cultures	食品文化	shípǐn wénhuà
1998	foods that constitute meals	膳食组成食品	shànshí zǔchéng shípǐn
1998	fortification of foods	食品营养素增加	shípǐn yíngyǎngsù zēngjiā
1998	fortified foods	强化食品	qiánghuà shípǐn
2003	foods from 'wild' sources	'野生'资源食品	'yěshēng' zīyuán shípǐn
2003	low energy-dense (or energy-dilute) foods	低能量 (弱能量) 食品	dī néngliàng (ruò néngliàng) shípǐn
1998	natural foods	自然食品	zìrán shípǐn
1998	protective foods	保护性食品	bǎohù xìng shípǐn
1998	designer foods	设计者食品	shèjì zhě shípǐn
Foods translated as '膳食' (shànshí)			
1998	food-based guidelines	膳食指南	shànshí zhǐnán
1998	food-based guidelines	膳食指导	shànshí zhǐdǎo
2003	globalization of foods	膳食全球化	shànshí quánqiú huà
2003	healthy foods	健康膳食	jiànkāng shànshí
1998	fortification of complementary foods	辅食强化	fǔshí qiánghuà

Note: Lexical variation in the translation of food schema in nutrition research

Appendix 7

Food grouping schema – translation of culturally based dietary pattern research (1)

Date	Original English expression	Chinese translation	Pinyin annotation
2003	food items	食品分类	shípǐn fēnlèi
2003	food labeling	食品标识	shípǐn biāozhì
1998	food lists	食品目录	shípǐn mùlù
1998	food patterns	食品模式	shípǐn móshì
1998	food patterns	食品类型	shípǐn lèixíng
1998	food tables	食品表	shípǐn biǎo
1998	food variety indices	食品多样化指标	shípǐn duōyàng huà zhǐbiāo
1998	food classification systems	食品分类	shípǐn fēnlèi
1998	food combinations	食品结合	shípǐn jiéhé
1998	food combinations	结合性膳食	jiéhé xìng shànshí
1998	food consumption	食品消耗	shípǐn xiāohào
2003	food consumption pattern	粮食消费模式	Liángshí xiāofèi móshì
1998	food consumption patterns	食品食用模式	shípǐn shíyòng móshì
1998	food consumption patterns	食品消耗模式	shípǐn xiāohào móshì
1998	hard-to-categorise foods	难分类食品	nán fēnlèi shípǐn

Note: Lexical variation in the translation of food schema in nutrition research

Appendix 8
Food grouping schema – translation of culturally based dietary pattern research (2)

Date	Original English expression	Chinese translation	Pinyin annotation
1998	food grouping schemes	食品分类方案	shípǐn fēnlèi fāng'àn
1998	food groupings	食品种类	Shípǐnzhǒnglèi
1998	food groups	食品类别	shípǐn lèibié
1998	food groups	普通食物	pǔtōng shíwù
1998	food groups	食品种类	shípǐn zhǒnglèi
1998	food groups	食品组	shípǐn zǔ
2003	food groups	食品组	shípǐn zǔ
1998	individual foods	单一食品	dānyī shípǐn
1998	individual foods	个别食品	gèbié shípǐn
1998	individual foods	单个食品	dāngè shípǐn

Note: Lexical variation in the translation of food schema in nutrition research

Appendix 9

Sugars – translation of sugar research terms (1)

Date	Original English expression	Chinese translation	Pinyin annotation
'Free'			
1990	free sugars	高简单糖类	Gāo jiǎndān táng lèi
1990	free sugars	简单糖类	jiǎndān táng lèi
1990	free sugars	简单型糖类	jiǎndān xíng táng lèi
2003	free sugars	游离糖	yóulí tang
2003	free sugars in beverages	饮料中游离糖	yǐnliào zhōng yóulí táng
1998	simple carbohydrates	单糖	dān tang
1998	simple sugar	单糖	dān tang
1998	simple sugars	单纯糖类	dānchún táng lèi
1990	intake of free sugars	简单糖类摄入量	jiǎndān táng lèi shè rù liàng
'Complex'			
1998	complex carbohydrate	多糖	Duōtáng
1998	complex carbohydrate	复合碳水化合物	fùhé tànshuǐ huàhéwù
Plurality			
1998b	galactose	半乳糖	bàn rǔtáng
1998a	monosaccharides	单糖	dān tang
2003	monosaccharides	单糖	dān tang
1998a	oligosaccharides	寡糖	guǎ tang
1998a	disaccharides	双糖	shuāng táng
2003	disaccharides	二糖	èr tang
2003	non-starch polysaccharides	非淀粉多糖	fēi diànfěn duōtáng
1998b	polysaccharides	多糖	Duōtáng

Note: Lexical variation in the translation of sugar research terms

Appendix 10
Sugars – translation of sugar research terms (2)

Date	Original English expression	Chinese translation	Pinyin annotation
1998	glycaemic effect	血糖效应	xiětáng xiàoyìng
1998	retarded glycaemic effect	迟发型血糖效应	chí fǎxíng xiětáng xiàoyìng
2003	glucose intolerance	葡萄糖不耐性	pútáotáng bù nàixìng
1998	glucose tolerance	葡萄糖耐量	pútáotáng nàiliàng
2003	hereditary fructose intolerance	遗传性果糖不耐受性	yíchuán xìng guǒtáng bù nài shòu xìng
2003	impaired glucose tolerance	糖耐量受损	táng nàiliàng shòu sǔn
1998	lactose tolerance	乳糖耐量	rǔtáng nàiliàng
1998	low-glycaemic-index foods	低糖指数食品	dītáng zhǐshù shípǐn
1990	glucose	葡萄糖	Pútáotáng
1998	glycaemic index	血糖指数	xiětáng zhǐshù
1990	glycogen	糖原	táng yuán
1998	glycoproteins	糖蛋白	táng dànbái
2003	impaired glucose tolerance	糖耐量受损	táng nàiliàng shòu sǔn
1998	impaired glucose tolerance	糖耐量减低	táng nàiliàng jiǎndī

Note: Lexical variation in the translation of sugar research terms

Appendix 11

Translation and use of adjectives in medical terms

Date	Original English expression	Chinese translation	Pinyin annotation
'Central'			
2003	central adiposity	中部肥胖	Zhōngbù féipàng
2003	central obesity	中等肥胖	zhōngděng féipàng
'Complex'			
1998	complex carbohydrate	多糖	Duōtáng
1998	complex carbohydrate	复合碳水化合物	fùhé tànshuǐ huàhéwù
1990	complex carbohydrate foods	复合碳水化合物食物	fùhé tànshuǐ huàhéwù shíwù
1998	complex carbohydrates	完全碳水化合物	wánquán tànshuǐ huàhéwù
1998	complex carbohydrates	复合碳水化合物	fùhé tànshuǐ huàhéwù
1998	complex glyco-conjugates	复合葡萄糖结合物	fùhé pútáotáng jiéhé wù
2003	complex mixture	复杂综合作用	fùzá zònghé zuòyòng
'Macro-'			
1998	macrobiotic diets	长寿膳食 (节食)	Chángshòu shànshí (jiéshí)
1990	macronutrient composition	常量营养素构成	chángliàng yíngyǎngsù gòuchéng
1998	macronutrient content of complementary foods	辅食的宏量营养素含量	fùshí de hóng liàng yíngyǎngsù hánliàng
1998	macronutrients	常量营养素	chángliàng yíngyǎngsù
1998	macronutrients	宏量营养素	hóng liàng yíngyǎngsù
1998	macronutrients	宏量营养素	hóng liàng yíngyǎngsù
2003	macronutrients	大量营养素	dàliàng yíngyǎngsù
2003	macronutrients	大量营养素	dàliàng yíngyǎngsù

Note: Lexical variation in the translation of adjectives in health research terms

Appendix 12
Translation of health research methodology

Date	Original English expression	Chinese translation	Pinyin annotation
'Cross-sectional'			
1998	cross-sectional comparison	横断面对比	Héngduàn miàn duì bǐ
1998	cross-sectional studies	横断面研究	héngduàn miàn yánjiū
2003	cross-sectional studies	跨部门研究	kuà bùmén yánjiū
'Independent'			
1998	independent risk factor	独立危险因子	Dúlì wéixiǎn yīnzǐ
2003	independent risk factor for CVD	心血管病的独立因素	xīn xiěguǎn bìng de dúlì yīnsù
1998	Independently identify	独立发现	dúlì fāxiàn
2003	independently to predict CHD	独立地预示冠心病	dúlì dì yùshì guàn xīnbìng
'Longitudinal'			
1998	longitudinal data	纵向资料	Zòngxiàng zīliào
2003	longitudinal studies	连续性研究	liánxù xìng yánjiū
1998	longitudinal study	纵向研究	zòngxiàng yánjiū

Note: Lexical variation in the translation of health research methodologies

Appendix 13

Translation of nutrition recommendations (1)

Date	Original English expression	Chinese translation	Pinyin annotation
'Required'			
1998	required nutrient intakes	基础营养摄入	Jīchǔ yíngyǎng shè rù
1998	required nutrient intakes	基础营养摄入	jīchǔ yíngyǎng shè rù
1998	requirements for all essential nutrients	必需营养素的需要量	bìxū yíngyǎngsù de xūyào liàng
1998	amino acid requirements	氨基酸需要量	ānjīsuān xūyào liàng
1998	nutrient requirement	营养需要量	yíngyǎng xūyào liàng
1998	nutritional requirements	营养需要量	yíngyǎng xūyào liàng
'Desired'			
1998	desirable nutrient intakes	必需营养摄入	Bìxū yíngyǎng shè rù
1998	desirable range of intake	必需摄入范围	bìxū shè rù fànwéi
1998	desired content and density of nutrients	营养素理想含量和密度	yíngyǎngsù lǐxiǎng hánliàng hé mìdù
1998	desired intake	期望摄入量	qīwàng shè rù liàng
1998	desired intakes	理想的摄入	lǐxiǎng de shè rù
'Essential'			
1998	conditionally essential amino acids	条件性必需氨基酸	Tiáojiàn xìng bìxū ānjīsuān
1990	essential amino acids	必需氨基酸	bìxū ānjīsuān
1998	essential fatty acids	必需脂肪酸	bìxū zhīfángsuān
1998	essential fatty acids	必需脂肪酸	bìxū zhīfángsuān
1990	essential nutrients	必需营养素	bìxū yíngyǎngsù
1998	essential nutrients	基本营养素	jīběn yíngyǎngsù
1998	essential nutrients	必需营养素	bìxū yíngyǎngsù
1990	essential structural fatty acids	必需结构脂肪酸	bìxū jiégòu zhīfángsuān

Note: Lexical variation in the translation of nutrition recommendations

Appendix 14

Translation of nutrition recommendations (2)

Date	Original English expression	Chinese translation	Pinyin annotation
'Exclusive'			
1998	exclusivity of breast-feeding	纯母乳喂养程度	Chún mǔrǔ wèiyǎng chéngdù
1998	almost exclusive breast-feeding	几乎完纯母乳喂养	jīhū wán chún mǔrǔ wèiyǎng
1998	full breast-feeding	充足母乳喂养	chōngzú mǔrǔ wèiyǎng
1998	full breast-feeding	全母乳喂养	quán mǔrǔ wèiyǎng
1998	partial breast-feeding	部分母乳喂养	bùfèn mǔrǔ wèiyǎng
'Total'			
1998	total diet	整个膳食	Zhěnggè shànshí
1998	total diet	全部膳食	quánbù shànshí
1998	total diet	总体膳食	zǒngtǐ shànshí
1998	total diet	总体膳食	zǒngtǐ shànshí
'Optimal'			
1998	optimal	最适宜	zuì shìyí
1998	optimal duration	适宜持续时间	shìyí chíxù shíjiān
1998	optimal duration	最佳持续时间	zuì jiā chíxù shíjiān
1998	optimal feeding	最适宜喂养	zuì shìyí wèiyǎng
1998	optimal nutrient intake	合理营养摄入	hélǐ yíngyǎng shè rù
'Appropriate'			
1998	appropriate diets	合理膳食	Hélǐ shànshí
1998	appropriate energy density	合适的能量密度	héshì de néngliàng mìdù

Note: Lexical variation in the translation of nutrition recommendations

Bibliography

Al-Amer, R., Ramjan, L., Glew, P., Darwish, M., and Salamonson, Y. (2015). Translation of interviews from a source language to a target language: Examining issues in cross-cultural health care research. *Journal of Clinical Nursing*, 24(9–10), 1151–1162.

Anthony, L. (2013). A critical look at software tools in corpus linguistics. *Linguistic Research*, 30(2), 141–161.

AUSDIAB: The Australian Diabetes, Obesity and Lifestyle Study (2012), Victoria, Australia: Baker Heart and Diabetes Institute.

Australian Bureau of Statistics (2014–15). *Migration in Australia.* www.abs.gov.au/ausstats/abs@.nsf/lookup/3412.0Media%20Release12014-15

Barber, S.L., Borowitz, M., Bekedam, H., and Ma, J. (2013). The hospital of the future in China: China's reform of public hospitals and trends from industrialized countries. *Health Policy and Planning*, czt023.

Baumann, K.-D. (2007). "A Communicative – Cognitive Approach to Emotion in LSP Communication." In A. Khurshid and M. Rogers (eds.), *Evidence-Based LSP: Translation, Text and Terminology* (323–344). Oxford: Peter Lang.

Bowker, L. and Pearson, J. (2002). *Working with Specialized Language: A Practical Guide to Using Corpora.* London and New York: Routledge.

Chen, H.C. and Ng, M.L. (1989). Semantic facilitation and translation priming effects in Chinese-English bilinguals. *Memory and Cognition*, July 1, 17(4), 454–462.

Chen, J., Hou, X. and Zhao, W. (2016). Research on the model of consumer health information seeking behavior via social media. *International Journal of Communications, Network and System Sciences*, 9(8), 326.

Kristine Aquino (2015). *Cultural and Linguistic Diversity in Greater Western Sydney.* Parramatta, NSW: Westir Ltd.

Delavari, A., A, Forouzanfar MH, Alikhani S, Sharifian A, Kleishadi R. (2009). First nationwide study of the prevalence of the metabolic syndrome and optimal cutoff points of waist circumference in the Middle East. *The National Survey of Risk Factors for Non-Communicable Diseases of Iran*, 32(6), 1092–1097.

Demmen, J. E., Semino, E., Demjen, Z., Koller, V., Hardie, A., Rayson, P., & Payne, S. (2015). A computer-assisted study of the use of violence metaphors for cancer and end of life by patients, family carers and health professionals. *International Journal of Corpus Linguistics*, 20(2), 205–231.

Diabetes Australia (2010). *The Glycaemic Index*. https://static.diabetesaustralia.com.au/s/fileassets/diabetes-australia/233f347d-3a90-4cd7-b429-c25842ba6193.pdf

Diabetes Australia (2013). *National Diabetes Strategy and Action Plan Federal Election*. Canberra: ACT, Australia

Diabetes NSW (2012). The glycemic index. *Talking Diabetes*, 17 (revised version).

Field, A. (2000). *Discovering Statistics Using SPSS for Windows*. London: Sage Publications.

Field, A. (2009). *Discovering Statistics Using SPSS*. London: Sage Publications.

Fischbach, H. (1998). Translation and medicine. *American Translators Association Series X*, 1–12.

Gerzymisch-Arbogast, H. (2007). "Fundamentals of LSP Translation." In H. Gerzymisch-Arbogast, G. Budin and G. Hofer (eds.), *LSP Translation Scenarios: MuTra Journal*, 2, 7–64. Honolulu, HI: The ATRC Group

Global Health Data Exchange. http://ghdx.healthdata.org/gbd-results-tool

Gravetter, F. and Wallnau, L. (2014). *Essentials of Statistics for the Behavioral Sciences* (8th ed.). Belmont, CA: Wadsworth.

Harkness, J., Pennell, B.E., Villar, A., Gebler, N., Aguilar-Gaxiola, S., Bilgen, I., Kessler, R.C., and Üstün, T.B. (2008). Translation procedures and translation assessment in the World Mental Health Survey Initiative. *The WHO World Mental Health Surveys: Global Perspectives on the Epidemiology of Mental Disorders*, 91–113.

Hook, G., Lester, L., Ji, M., Edney, K., Pope, C., and van der Does-Ishikawa, L. (2017). *Environmental Pollution and the Media: Political Discourses of Risk and Responsibility in Australia, China and Japan*. London: Routledge.

House, J. (2008). "Intercultural Discourse and Translation." In H. Gerzymisch-Arbogast, G. Budin and G. Hofer (eds.), *LSP Translation Scenarios: MuTra Journal*, 2, 109–130. Honolulu, HI: The ATRC Group.

Hsieh, E. (2016). *Bilingual Health Communication: Working with Interpreters in Cross-Cultural Care*. London: Routledge.

Huff, R.M., Kline, M. V., & Peterson, D. V. eds. (2014). *Health Promotion in Multicultural Populations*. Thousand Oaks, CA: Sage Publications.

Hunt, D. and Harvey, K. (2015). "Health Communication and Corpus Linguistics: Using Corpus Tools to Analyse Eating Disorder Discourse Online." In *Corpora and Discourse Studies*, 134–154. London: Palgrave Macmillan.

Ji, M., ed. (2016). *Empirical Translation Studies: An Interdisciplinary Approach*. Sheffield: Equinox.

Ji, M., Hareide, L., Li, D., Oakes, M. (2016). *Corpus Methodologies Explained: An Empirical Approach to Translation Studies*. Abingdon: Routledge.

Laviosa, S., Pagano, A., Kemppanen, H., Ji, M. (2016). *Textual and Contextual Analysis in Empirical Translation Studies*. New York: Springer.

Li, L.I.U. (2007). Further exploitation and utilization of the retrieval function of CNKI [J]. *Journal of Academic Library and Information Science*, 1, 14.

Lin, S. and Ji, M. (2017). *Using social media platform for multicultural T2D health education*, Presentation at the 34th National Conference of the Dietitians Association of Australia, Hobart, Tasmania.

Michie, S., van Stralen, M.M., and West, R. (2011). The behaviour change wheel: A new method for characterising and designing behaviour change interventions. *Implementation Science*, 6(1), 42.

Moorhead, S.A., Hazlett D. E., Harrison L., Carroll J. K., Irwin A., Hoving C. (2013). A new dimension of health care: Systematic review of the uses, benefits, and limitations of social media for health communication. *Journal of Medical Internet Research*, 15(4).

Morony, S., Kleitman, S., Lee, Y. P., & Stankov, L. (2013). Predicting achievement: Confidence vs. self-efficacy, anxiety, and self-concept in Confucian and European countries. *International Journal of Educational Research*, 58, 79–96.

Multi-Sectoral Action and Partnerships for Non-Communicable Diseases (2012). Australian Government Submission to the World Health Organization (WHO). www.health.gov.au/internet/main/publishing.nsf/Content/sfwnc

Murray, C.J. and A.D. Lopez' (eds.) (1996) *The Global Burden of Disease: a comprehensive assessment of mortality and disability from diseases, injuries, and risk factors in 1990 and projected to 2020.* Boston, MA: Harvard School of Public Health on behalf of the World Health Organization and the World Bank.

Ng, M., Fleming, T., Robinson, M., Thomson, B., Graetz, N., Margono, C., Mullany, E.C., Biryukov, S., Abbafati, C., Abera, S.F., and Abraham, J.P. (2014). Global, regional, and national prevalence of overweight and obesity in children and adults during 1980–2013: A systematic analysis for the Global Burden of Disease Study 2013. *Lancet*, 384(9945), 766–781.

Nicholas, D.B., Fellner, K. D., Frank, M., Small, M., Hetherington, R., Slater, R., & Daneman, D. (2012). Evaluation of an online education and support intervention for adolescents with diabetes. *In Social Work in Health Care*, 51(9), 815–827.

Nutrition Australia (2009). *Carbohydrates and GI.* www.nutritionaustralia.org/national/resource/diabetes

Oakes, M., Bobicev, V., & Sokolova, M. (2015). Learning sentiments in online medical forums. *Cognitive Computation*, 7(5), 609–621.

Peng, R., Zhang, L., and Fan, Y. (2012). Comparison of international and Chinese food label legislation. *Chinese Food Health*, 24(3), 250–255.

Piao, S., Bianchi, F, Dayrell, C, D'egidio, A & Rayson, P (2015). *Development of the multilingual semantic annotation system*, Proceedings of the 2015 Conference of the North American Chapter of the Association for Computational Linguistics – Human Language Technologies, pp. 1268–1274.

Pietrzak, P. (2015). Stylistic aspects of English and Polish medical records. *The Journal of Specialised Translation*, 23, 316–332.

Potter, L., Wallston, K., Trief, P., Ulbrecht, J., Juth, V., & Smyth, J. (2015). Attributing discrimination to weight: Associations with well-being, self-care, and disease status in patients with type 2 diabetes mellitus. *Journal of Behavioral Medicine*, 38(6), 863–875.

Prasad, R., Webber, B., and Joshi, A. (2014). Reflections on the penn discourse treebank, comparable corpora, and complementary annotation. *Computational Linguistics*.

Schulz, P., Hartung, U., and Riva, S. (2013). Causes, coping, and culture: A comparative survey study on representation of back pain in three Swiss language regions. *PLoS One*, 8(11), e78029.

Schwartländer, B. (1997). Global burden of disease. *The Lancet*, 350(9071), 141–142.

Straus, S., Tetroe, J., and Graham, I.D., eds. (2013). *Knowledge Translation in Health Care: Moving from Evidence to Practice*. Hoboken, NJ: John Wiley & Sons, May 31.

Teich, E. (2003). Cross-linguistic variation in system and text: A methodology for the investigation of translations and comparable texts. *Walter de Gruyter*.

Trochim, W.M. and Donnelly, J.P. (2006). *The Research Methods Knowledge Base* (3rd ed.). Cincinnati, OH: Atomic Dog.

Wang, G. and Wang, L. (2015). Analysis on the results of agricultural science and technology literature retrieval based on CNKI, Wanfang and VIP retrieval platform. *Agriculture Network Information*, 7, 16.

Wang, L.B. (2008). Disease prevention and health industry development. *Global Traditional Chinese Medicine*, 1(2), 5–6.

Wang, X.H. (2015). Big Health Industry as the new economic growth point. *Law and Economy*, 10, 52.

Wang, Y. (2014). Health Industry, the fifth industrial wave: The next industrial growth underscored by the big health industry. *High-Tech and Industralisation*, 12, 32–37.

WHO (1998). *Preparation and Use of Food-Based Dietary Guidelines: Report of a Joint FAO/WHO Consultation*. Geneva, Switzerland.

WHO (2012). *Process of Translation and Adaptation of Instruments*. www.who.int/ substance_abuse/research_tools/translation/en/

World Health Organization (2000a). *Annual Report Health Systems: Improving Performance*. www.who.int/whr/2000/en/whr00_en.pdf

World Health Organization (2000b). *Annual Report She Jie Wei Sheng Bao Gao: Wei Sheng Xi Tong, Gai Jin Bao Gao*, translated by People's Health Press. Beijing: Chinese Ministry of Health.

Xu, M., Shi, L., and Yin, J. (2014). Encountermeasures to problems in food labelling. *Chinese Food and Nutrition*, 20(5), 10–12.

Zhang, J., Huang, F., Huo, F., and Zhang, B. (2015). Survey of knowledge, attitude and consumption behaviour of packaged food among Chinese city populations. *Chinese Food and Nutrition*, 21(2), 46–48.

Zheng, Q. and Jiang, S. (2013). *An online Chinese-English academic dictionary based on bilingual literature abstracts*, Information Science and Technology (ICIST), 2013 International Conference in Yangzhou, Jiangsu, China, on Mar 23, pp. 777–779. IEEE.

Index

Note: Page numbers in italic indicate a figure and page numbers in bold indicate a table on the corresponding page.